SCORING

for the

BAND

By

Philip J. Lang

Belwin Mills Publishing Corp.

90078

The author gratefully acknowledges the invaluable assistance of William D. Revelli, University of Michigan, and Walter Beeler, Ithaca College; for their help and interest in the preparation and laboratoring of this book.

The author gratefully acknowledges the invaluable assistance of William D. Revelli, University of Michigan, and Walter Beeler, Ithaca College; for their help and interest in the preparation and laboratoring of this book.

A complete listing of musical references with their proper credit appears on page 214.

Produced in the United States of America

TABLE OF CONTENTS

PART FOUR

TYPES OF BAND SCORING

INTRODUCTION

It is not the purpose of this book to teach the fundamentals of music. Orchestration is one of the highest branches of musical art and should not be attempted until a reasonably fair background in the foundations of music has been realized. It is not possible to write for any group of instruments, or successfully attempt the study of orchestration, without a complete working knowledge of the theory of music. The mundane basic lessons of music are of the utmost importance to the orchestrator, and many famous orchestrators have reopened their first primers in an effort to further their technique.

Theory, harmony, and the notation of music are the tools of the art. No one must know them as well, or use them as often, as the orchestrator. Technique is all-important in writing for instruments and is exhibited by the worker facile in the use of his tools. Key signatures, clefs, scales, chord construction, and inversions are some of the elementary knowledge required. Familiarization with, and understanding of, counterpoint, and canon and fugue is necessary for advanced work. If the reader is not sure of this material he would do well to brush up on it or avail himself of a good textbook to use in conjunction with this study.

Since orchestration is the art of writing for instruments, the ability to recognize instrumental timbre is important. The tonal qualities of all instruments throughout their registers should be readily distinguished. Each instrument of the band should be recognized whether heard singly, or in combination. The middle tones of a clarinet should not be confused with the low tones of a flute, nor those of the horn with the trombone. Careful listening to instrumental music will quickly develop the ability to distinguish the different solo instruments and penetrate complex orchestral colors to detect the component instruments.

For the orchestrator, this faculty must be developed to an imaginative extent. It is necessary to hear in your mind's ear the tone of an instrument or combination of instruments. Scoring for instruments is a hit and miss proposition unless the timbres can be heard in the mind. A little exercise in mentally scoring the melody of some simple tune such as "Swanee River," for oboe, bassoon, or trombone, will quickly develop this faculty. If some instrumental tone persists in being elusive make an early effort to etch it in your mind by personal use of the instrument, or seek it on records, or at concerts.

The ability to play an instrument, or instruments, is required of an orchestrator. Playing with a band or orchestra provides close contact with all the families of instruments. Be observant! A short discussion with a bassoon player is worth more than studying all the books ever written about the instrument. Make friends with and ask questions of your fellow musicians, and you will be greatly rewarded. Request them to play scales, trills, and demonstrate technique with their favorite passages. Knowledge that the clarinet range is from low E to a possible high A, and a middle B-flat to B trill very difficult is hardly sufficient knowledge to intelligently write for the instrument. What are the tonal qualities of its highest, middle, and lowest register? How does its volume compare with that of other woodwinds? With brasses? How is its legato and staccato?

These, and hundreds of others, are the facts you should seek and know. Whenever possible, try to familiarize yourself with as many instruments as you can. Know the basic fingerings, register changes and slide positions of all instruments. This knowledge will enable you to grasp a ruler, and by placing your fingers on it, quickly check the fingering of any passage you may be writing.

Learn to read from a score. Familiarize yourself with the standard score page for band and orchestra. Develop the ability to visually divide the page into sections for brass, reeds, and percussion; then further divide each section into its component instruments. Be able to find each instrument with a quick glance at the page, and not have to use your forefinger in the left margin.

When writing for band, set up the score page in the proper manner from the very first exercise. Allow room above and below the staff for each instrument and make an orderly division for each instrumental family. Temperament and sloppiness have no place in orchestration. Your scores must be readable as well as playable. Countless good orchestrations have been discarded because the conductor could not decipher the score.

Since the purpose of this book is to instruct in scoring for band, the subject of instrumentation will be treated very briefly. Whole volumes could be devoted to this subject, and there are many excellent ones available. The enclosed chapter on instrumentation, while complete and up-to-date, is offered as a guide and reference with the hope that the reader will personally pursue this important study by contact with instruments and their performers.

Beginning with Part Two of this book, work projects in scoring are indicated in the text by the symbol **WP** *. These exercises are progressive, designed to insure understanding and use of each device and technique of scoring,* as presented, and before proceeding to the next. The maximum value of this study will be realized only by the execution of each and every one of these projects as they are indicated. Whenever possible, these projects, even the simplest, should be played by the instruments for which they are scored. Only by hearing the actual sound of his efforts can the student evaluate his progress and technique.[1]

For the instructor, using this book as a text, the author feels (contrary to general procedure) it is not necessary that the subject of Instrumentation (Part 1) be completely mastered before attempting scoring. No one studying orchestration, or engaged in scoring, ever ceases to study Instrumentation. Insistance upon complete mastery of this subject as a prerequisite to scoring results in a superficial rote memorizing, and subsequent lack of interest, in this vital (and eventually very interesting) phase of scoring.

Parts Two and Three of this book should receive the major share of instruction, discussion and class periods. The recommended distribution is as follows:

Part One—Instrumentation.............................One/Sixth of Class Periods
Part Two—Instrumental Voices.....................One/Third of Class Periods
Part Three—Devices, Techniques.................One/Third of Class Periods
Part Four—Types of Scoring........................One/Sixth of Class Periods

It is obvious that the time devoted to Part Four will depend upon the advancement of the class, and the speed with which they absorb the techniques and devices. Part One will be a constant factor, and source of discussion throughout this entire study.

---

1. For these projects the student should be provided with a looseleaf binder using ten or twelve staff manuscript paper, and suitable band full score paper (or blank mms. with sufficient staves to make his own). The projects should be kept in order with the small ensemble projects executed on the mms. paper and the full score projects inserted in order after being folded in half and punched.

GENERAL INFORMATION

The instruments comprising the band are divided into three families: Woodwinds, Brass, and Percussion. Each family is composed as follows:

Ex. 1

WOODWINDS

Piccolos (C and D-flat)	Treble Clef
Flute (C)	Treble Clef
²Alto Flute (G)	Treble Clef
Oboe (C)	Treble Clef
English Horn (F)	Treble Clef
E-flat Clarinet	Treble Clef
B-flat Clarinet	Treble Clef
E-flat Alto Clarinet	Treble Clef
B-flat Bass Clarinet	Treble Clef
²B-flat Contra Bass Clarinet	Treble Clef
Bassoon (C)	Bass Clef—Tenor Clef—Treble Clef
²Contra Bassoon (C)	Bass Clef
E-flat Alto Saxophone	Treble Clef
B-flat Tenor Saxophone	Treble Clef
E-flat Baritone Saxophone	Treble Clef
²B-flat Bass Saxophone	Treble Clef

BRASS

²Cornet (E-flat)	Treble Clef
Cornet (B-flat)	Treble Clef
Trumpet (B-flat)	Treble Clef
²Fluegelhorn (B-flat)	Treble Clef
French Horn (F)	Treble Clef
Alto Horn (E-flat)	Treble Clef (Mellophone)
Trombone (C)	Bass Clef
Bass Trombone (C)	Bass Clef
Baritone (C)	Bass Clef—Treble Clef (Tenor Clef)
Euphonium (C)	Bass Clef—Treble Clef (Tenor Clef)
E-flat Tuba (C)	Bass Clef
Tuba (B-flat) (C)	Bass Clef

PERCUSSION TUNED

Marimba (C)	Treble Clef
Xylophone (C)	Treble Clef
Chimes (C)	Treble Clef
Steel Bells (C)	Treble Clef
Tympani (C)	Bass Clef

UNTUNED

Snare Drum, Bass Drum, Cymbals, Triangle, Wood Blocks, etc.

2. Instruments not commonly used in the band.

Occasionally other instruments viz: string bass, cello, harp, accordion, etc., are added to the band. These instruments and their usage will be discussed later. Also, later on in this study, it will be apparent that some of the above instruments have seemingly outlived their usefulness, and are in the process of being eliminated from the band.

In charting the registers, limitations, and possibilities of the individual instruments comprising the band, the terms "Concert" and "Transposing" will be used frequently. These terms and their use must be clearly understood. Some of the instruments of the band are Concert instruments, and others are Transposing instruments. Reference to Ex. 1 will show some instruments designated as "B-flat," "E-flat," and "F," while others are not so designated. When a flute plays "C" on his instrument, it is the same pitch as the same register "C" on the piano. Therefore, the flute is in concert with the piano and is designated as a "Concert" instrument. When the clarinet plays "C" on his instrument it is the same as "B-flat" (a whole tone lower) on the piano. To compensate for this difference all music for the clarinet is written one whole tone higher. Therefore, the clarinet is designated as a "Transposing" instrument in "B-flat." Similarly, the tone "C" on a French horn is the same as "F" (a fifth lower) on the piano. This designates the French horn as an "F" instrument and all its music is written a fifth higher. The alto saxophone "C" is the same as the "E-flat" (a sixth lower) on the piano. All music for the alto saxophone is written a sixth higher and the instrument is said to be in "E-flat."

A simple rule for the complete understanding of transposition is as follows: ALL TRANSPOSING INSTRUMENTS (except the D-flat piccolo, E-flat cornet, and E-flat clarinet) are pitched *BELOW* middle "C." To write for these instruments it is necessary to bring their pitch *UP* to middle "C." All "B-flat" instruments[3] are one whole tone below middle "C" and have to be written one whole tone higher. All "F" instruments are a fifth lower and all "E-flat" instruments[4] are a sixth lower. These instruments have to be written respectively, a fifth and a sixth higher. The "D-flat" piccolo and the "E-flat" clarinet and "E-flat" cornet are respectively a half tone and a tone and a half *ABOVE* middle "C." These instruments are the only exceptions to the above rule, and as a result are written *down* the corresponding interval.

Some instruments of the band are further written an octave higher, in addition to their transposition. This is no violation of the above rule but is a compensation for the clef used for their music. Complete information of these instruments will be presented in the chapter on instrumentation.

---

3. The B-flat Tenor Saxophone is a tone and an *additional* octave below middle "C."
4. The E-flat Baritone Saxophone is a sixth and an *additional* octave below middle "C."

6

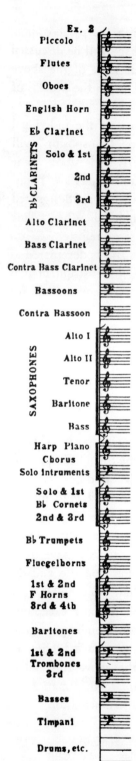

Ex. 2

Piccolo

Flutes

Oboes

English Horn

Eb Clarinet

Bb CLARINETS
Solo & 1st

2nd

3rd

Alto Clarinet

Bass Clarinet

Contra Bass Clarinet

Bassoons

Contra Bassoon

SAXOPHONES
Alto I

Alto II

Tenor

Baritone

Bass

Harp Piano
Chorus
Solo Intruments

Solo & 1st
Bb Cornets
2nd & 3rd

Bb Trumpets

Fluegelborns

1st & 2nd
F Horns
3rd & 4th

Baritones

1st & 2nd
Trombones
3rd

Basses

Timpani

Drums, etc.

Ex. 2 is a marginal section of the proper instrumental layout of the full band score page. It lists all the instruments of the band in the proper score order and the correct clefs for each. Constant reference to this Ex. is suggested in executing all scoring exercises to establish the habit of using the correct score layout.

Part One
INSTRUMENTATION

INSTRUMENTATION

FLUTES AND PICCOLOS

The flute is a concert instrument and is always written in the treble clef. Its compass is as follows:

The upper C is also possible but uncertain, and should not be written. The upper B and B-flat are also very difficult and should be avoided whenever possible.

The flute is the most agile of all the wind instruments in the band. In familiar keys, not more than three sharps or flats, rapid passages can be easily executed, both legato and staccato. It is particularly adapted to this latter facility due to its ease of "double-tongueing."[6] Throughout the compass of the flute all the tones are even, and there is no noticeable change of register. The upper register is brilliant and penetrating, while the lower is resonant but weak. In solo passages the flute is highly effective, due to its facility, expressiveness, and extreme compass. The extract below will illustrate the delicacy of this instrument.

The most common use of the flute in the band is in strengthening the oboe and clarinet by doubling these instruments in unison or the octave.

---

5. The dotted lines indicate the best practical compass for ensemble scoring.
6. A rapid movement of the tongue against the roof of the mouth.

Ex. 4

Due to the facility of the flute and its brilliance in the upper register it is valuable for playing figures.

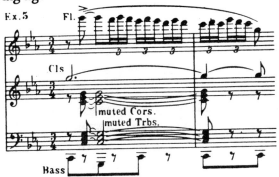

Ex. 5

The ability of the flute to execute long trills is an effect of great brilliance, and has ample power to dominate, even when scored against the full band.

Ex. 6

Two flutes as a duet or three as a trio are by turns gay, light, and playful, or shrill and brilliant. Melodic passages or figures are equally charming and effective.

Flutes can be utilized for many special or characteristic effects. The following extract from the "Yuletide Overture" is an example of flutes executing opposite trills to give the effect of sleighbells.

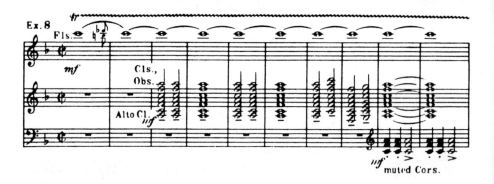

Later in the same composition the flutes are given a figure to heighten the effect of a gay party sleigh riding in the snow.

Repetition of rhythmic figures is also effective to create a mood of tension as in the "American Salute" passage below. The extreme contrast between the high flutes and the low bassoons creates a cold, ominous setting.

Ex.10

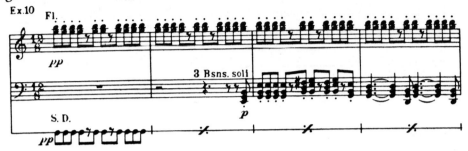

G ALTO FLUTE

Sometimes erroneously referred to as the bass flute, this is a transposing instrument in G and is always written in the treble clef. Its compass is as follows:

It is regrettable that this instrument is quite rare and while occasionally used in the orchestra, it is seldom, if ever, used in the band.[7]

In construction the Alto flute is similar to the C flute, although a trifle larger. The tone quality is rich and full. The Alto flute is used mostly in the lower register where the C flute is weak.

7. Publications for the band do not include a part for the Alto Flute.

C PICCOLO

The C piccolo is a concert instrument and is always written in the treble clef an octave lower than it sounds.[8] Its compass is as follows:

The piccolo is capable of the highest notes in the band. The notes of the low octave are very weak and are better played by the flute. The notes of the middle octave are more powerful, while those above —

are so piercing that they should be used with great care.

Solo passages are quite rare for this instrument although it has almost all the facility of the flute.

The chief use of the piccolo in the band is in doubling the flute or clarinet an octave higher.

Ex. 11

The addition of the piccolo to the flute in the execution of figures and trills strengthens the brilliance and power of these passages.

---

8. As practically the entire compass of this instrument is above the staff, it is obvious that if its music were not written an octave lower, the performer would always be looking for his notes amid countless ledger lines.

Ex.12

Piccolos also join the flutes in many characteristic effects. The military coloring of the "British Grenadiers" section in the "Salute To The Allies" is created by the use of flutes and piccolos in octaves.

Ex.13

Due to its powerful and piercing quality, the piccolo should be used with discretion. Overindulgence in the use of this instrument will nullify its effect, and create an impression of sameness and monotony.

D-FLAT PICCOLO

The D-flat piccolo is essentially the same as the C piccolo in every respect except that it is a transposing instrument in D-flat. It is always written in the treble clef and its compass is as follows:

This is one of the few instruments that violate the general rule[9] in that it is transposed one-half tone *down*. It is then written down an additional octave like the C piccolo.

The D-flat piccolo is usually used interchangeably with the C piccolo for facility in difficult keys. Passages for the C piccolo in the key of B, D-flat, and E, are simple for the D-flat piccolo, being respectively B-flat, C, and E-flat.

All references to the C piccolo, as regards use and tonal characterizations, are applicable to the D-flat piccolo.

9. See General Information.

OBOE

The oboe is a concert instrument and is always written in the treble clef. Its compass is as follows:

WRITTEN
and
SOUNDS

Some oboes also possess the lower B-flat but this note, as well as the B natural, is seldom written for the instrument. The upper E and F are very difficult to produce and are rarely used, except for solo passages or special effects. For general writing it is best to limit the upper register to D or E-flat.

There is an old axiom that "one should not write anything for the oboe that is not intended to be heard." The tone quality of this instrument is very pungent and distinctive, and its presence can readily be noted in almost any combination of instruments. The oboe is a facile instrument and most ordinary passages are easy but not all are effective. Care must be taken in writing for this instrument in assigning to it passages that are in keeping with its special peculiarities and distinctive quality of tone. The oboe is essentially a melodic instrument ideally suited for expressions of melancholy and tenderness.

Passages for other woodwinds, like the one below for clarinet,* would sound absurd if played by the oboe.

The expressiveness of this instrument and its distinctive quality of tone render it ideal for the many solo passages in band literature. Melodies of a sustained lyrical character and subtle dynamics are beautiful when scored for this instrument.

The same qualities are utilized in scoring countermelodies for the oboe.

The oboe is also very useful in combination with other woodwinds, both in unison and in the octave, by strengthening and imparting its distinctive color to the grouping.

Many novel effects are possible by the oboe both as a solo instrument, and in combination with others. It is most famous for its imitation of a duck "quack," and by burlesquing its melancholy character many other characterizations may be created.

ENGLISH HORN

The English Horn is a transposing instrument in F and is always written in the treble clef. Its compass is as follows:

This instrument is neither English nor a horn. It is a member of the double reed family and is actually an Alto oboe, bearing the same relationship to the oboe, as the Alto flute to the C flute. In construction it is similar to the oboe, differing only in that it is slightly larger, with an angled reed holder and a bulbous bell.

The tone of the English Horn resembles that of the oboe but is of a heavier, and thicker quality with a more dramatic character. It is used almost entirely as a solo instrument for the expression of dramatic melodies.

It is occasionally used to double other woodwinds both in unison and in the octave. A very effective double reed combination is achieved by the use of oboe and English Horn in octaves.

Like the oboe, care must be taken in scoring for this instrument only those passages that are suitable for its character.

BASSOON

The bassoon is a concert instrument and it is written in both the bass and the tenor clef.[10] Its compass is as follows:

WRITTEN
and
SOUNDS

In solo work the bassoon can ascend a few tones higher, but for general writing it is advisable not to go higher than the B-flat.

A member of the double reed family, the bassoon is the bass of the oboe as well as the bass to the whole woodwind group.[11] The compass of the instrument has different tonal qualities and may be divided into three registers. The low register is heavy and grotesque, the middle mournful and cold, and the high register expressive and lyrical, comparable to a tenor voice.

As a bass to the reed section, when a brass bass is undesirable, the bassoon has its greatest value. In the following excerpts it will be seen that if a tuba was used as a bass its volume and tone would be entirely out of proportion to the rest of the passage.

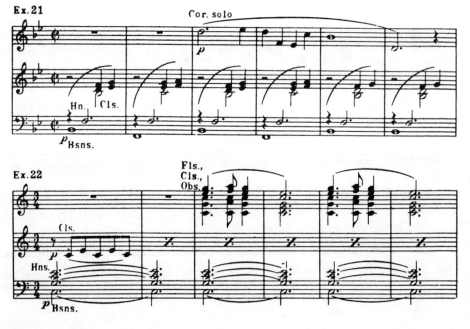

10. The tenor cleff is used for bassoon passages in the upper register to minimize the use of ledger lines.
11. In this capacity the bassoon is assisted by the bass clarinet.

As a bass instrument the bassoon is frequently added to the tuba in unison or the octave for reinforcement.

In unison with low register clarinets the tone of the bassoon adds strength and richness.

Due to its expressiveness the bassoon is valued as a solo instrument particularly in the middle and upper register. Here the instrument has a tonal quality that is very distinctive.

No other instrument is as capable of quick leaps of wide intervals as is the bassoon, and this facility is often used in accompaniments of an arpeggio nature.

12. Note the use of one trombone as a bass so that the weaker tone of the bassoon can predominate.

Ex.26

Two or three bassoons, soli, in duet, or trio form are particularly effective especially in passages of a staccato nature. In the following excerpt their dry, pungent quality imparts a feeling of virility and movement.

Ex.27

The bassoon has often been referred to as the "clown" of the orchestra due to its ability to be comic or grotesque.

CONTRA-BASSOON

The contra-bassoon is a concert instrument and is always written in the bass clef. Its compass is as follows:

This instrument, sometimes called the double-bassoon, is an octave lower than the bassoon and the lowest member of the double-reed family. In construction it is similar to the bassoon with larger tubing and an additional metal bell.

Because of its lack of agility, rapid movement is not possible, and only bass passages of moderate movement are playable.

The tone of the contra-bassoon is ponderous, sinister, and mournful.

This instrument is very rare and is present in only the large symphonic bands.[13] Its chief use is to reinforce the bass instruments.

---

13. Parts for the contra-bassoon are not included in published band arrangements.

B-FLAT CLARINET

The B-flat clarinet is a transposing instrument and is always written in the treble clef. Its compass is as follows:

For solo work the upper register can be extended a few tones, and in the hands of an expert performer a top C is possible. The very top notes are harsh, piercing and difficult to produce. For band writing, it is well to confine this instrument to the compass illustrated.

The compass of the clarinet can be divided into three separate registers, each possessing a slightly different quality of tone. The lowest register sometimes referred to as the "chalumeau"—

is very resonant, reedy, and is used for sustained tones and passages of moderate speed. Melodies in this register are particularly effective.

This register is also excellent for accompaniment figures, especially those of an arpeggio nature.

The second (middle) register —

is rich and full, similar to the flute tones, but more powerful. Here the clarinet has its greatest facility and the majority of its music is in this register.

Ex.31

The third (high) register —

is characterized by its strident quality. The notes are difficult to produce and uncertain in intonation. Fast chromatic passages in this register are difficult and precarious. However, this register has great value in tutti writing. Diatonic passages of moderate speed, utilizing the piercing quality of this register, are extremely effective.

The tones lying between the first and second registers —

re the weakest on the instrument. Due to the clarinet being constructed on a twelve tone harmonic system,[14] these notes bridge the gap between the first and second registers. This area is commonly referred to as the "bridge."[15] Passages of more than moderate speed in this area are difficult due to the fingering required for the change of register. Rapid playing of the following notes is difficult, but many alternate fingerings are available.

A clear knowledge of these three clarinet registers is important, and the following chart is offered for review.

---

14. All other woodwind instruments are constructed on an octave basis: the fingering for the first octave (eight tones) of the compass is, by the addition of the octave key, repeated for the second octave. The clarinet fingering is for the first twelve tones and then repeated.
15. Sometimes called "throat" register.

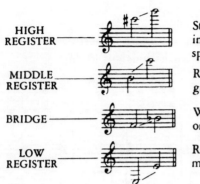

HIGH REGISTER		Strident quality. Difficult and uncertain of intonation except for passages of moderate speed.
MIDDLE REGISTER		Rich, full quality. Most useful register with greatest facility.
BRIDGE		Weak tones and awkward fingering. Use only for passages of moderate speed.
LOW REGISTER		Resonant, reedy quality. Sustained tones, melodies, and arpeggio figures.

Of all the woodwind instruments the clarinet possesses the greatest control of dynamics. The crescendo and diminuendo are much easier than on the flute, oboe, and bassoon, and can be carried to a greater extent. The faintest pianissimo is possible and is very effective when written for the entire clarinet section of the band.

The clarinets are the most important instruments of the band and the focal point of all scoring. The first clarinet bears the same relationship to the band as the first violin (concertmaster) does to the orchestra. All scoring for band is done with consideration of this family of instruments uppermost in mind. Selection of keys, distribution of melodies and counter-melodies is decided only after due consultation with the clarinet; the most tireless and indefatigable worker of the band.

The expressiveness and virtuosity of this instrument fully equip it as the leader in melodic scoring. Melodic passages for this instrument, either solo or the entire section in unison, abound in band literature. Passages in the upper register are brilliantly effective,

Ex.32 Cls.

while those utilizing the resonance of the lower register are warm and reedy.

Division of the clarinets into two, three, and even more parts is a common practice. The tonal blend is perfect, facility equal, and volume adequate.

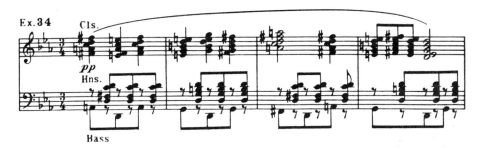

Technical passages of an ornamental nature (trills, quick runs, etc.) are well played and effective when scored for the clarinet.

Sustained harmony is excellent because of the dynamic flexibility of this instrument. Care has to be exercised in using this device in the low register as the reedy quality of the instrument is apt to sound muddy.

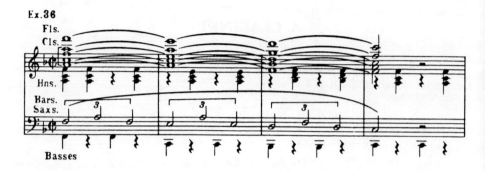

Ex. 36

Accompaniment figures in the lower and middle register, both legato and staccato, are ideal when scored for this instrument.

Ex. 37

Ex. 38

A CLARINET

The A clarinet is a transposing instrument and is always written in the treble clef. Its compass is as follows:

The A clarinet, like the D-flat piccolo, is used for greater ease in playing in sharp keys. The tone is a bit less brilliant than the B-flat clarinet.

Except for some very early publications, the A clarinet is not used in bands.[16] It is more often used in orchestra where most performers double on both B-flat and A clarinets.[17]

All references to the B-flat clarinet are applicable to the A clarinet, with the exception that all the registers are a half tone lower.

---

16. American publications for the band do not include a part for the A clarinet.
17. Even in the orchestra, it is the present custom to write, almost exclusively, for the B-flat clarinet. All references to the "clarinet," in band or orchestra, are understood to mean the instrument in B-flat.

E-FLAT CLARINET

The E-flat (small) clarinet is a transposing instrument[18] and is always written in the treble clef. Its compass is as follows:

The E-flat clarinet is almost exclusively a band instrument and is used to reinforce the flutes and the upper register of the B-flat clarinets.

The tones of the lower half of the compass are weak and this register is better played on the B-flat clarinet. In the upper register, where it is most frequently used, the E-flat clarinet has a shrill and piercing tone and the intonation is uncertain. These factors have resulted in a general dislike of the instrument, and it is gradually being replaced in the band by the addition of more flutes.

Like the flute, the E-flat clarinet is essentially a melodic instrument, and is valuable in reinforcing the flutes for a greater volume of tone.

Similarly it is used to strengthen the B-flat clarinets in the upper register.

---

18. The E-flat clarinet is one of the few instruments built *above* middle C and its music is transposed *down*.

Trills for piccolos and flutes are greatly increased in volume and intensity by the addition of the E-flat clarinet.

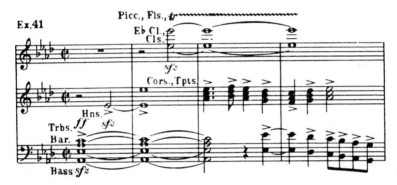

E-FLAT ALTO CLARINET

The E-flat alto clarinet is a transposing instrument and is always written in the treble clef.[19] Its compass is as follows:

While this instrument covers practically all vocal ranges (soprano, alto, tenor and bass) and is called an alto clarinet, it is used mostly in its tenor register.

The E-flat clarinet has great facility and a sonorous, reedy tone quality. It has tremendous possibilities as yet unrealized in the band, due to its being present in insufficient numbers. The average band has one or two alto clarinets whereas at least three, and preferably five, would be required for it to adequately perform its function as a tenor clarinet.

Solos for the alto clarinet are rare, its main function being one of reinforcement, particularly of the B-flat clarinets in the lower register.

Ex.42

Practically identical with the tonal quality of the bass clarinet, the alto clarinet is frequently used to double that instrument for greater strength.

Ex.43

Arpeggio accompaniments for the clarinets require the assistance of the alto clarinet to serve as a connection between the bass and B-flat clarinet.

19. Like the bass clarinet, the alto clarinet is sometimes written in the bass clef as a concert instrument. This practice is not recommended. The alto clarinet should be written in the treble clef as an E Flat instrument.

Ex.44

In full band scoring the alto clarinet is used to double other instruments, preferably reeds, in the tenor and alto register.

Ex.45

BASS CLARINET B-FLAT

The bass clarinet is a transposing instrument in B-flat and is always written in the treble clef.[20] Its compass is as follows:

This instrument is the bass of the clarinet family and assists the bassoon as the bass to the entire woodwind group. The bass clarinet has great facility and a beautiful mellow tone. Its legato in the bass register is a quality sorely needed in band scoring. Like the alto clarinet the possibilities of the bass clarinet have never been fully realized due to its presence in the band in insufficient numbers. Three or four bass clarinets are necessary to properly score for this instrument and permit it to be heard in proportion to the other clarinets.

As the average band rarely boasts of more than one bass clarinet it is seldom entrusted to melodic solos. While its facility and quality of tone are ideal for this purpose, great care has to be taken in scoring so that its relatively weak voice may be heard. The bass clarinet is more commonly used for light bass passages and figures. An excellent example of its best use is illustrated below where it is combined with bassoons.

It is occasionally used, in preference to the bassoon, as a bass to the clarinet family.

20. In German notation the bass clarinet is written in the bass clef as a concert instrument. This practice is outmoded and not recommended. As a B-flat instrument, music for the bass clarinet should be transposed up one tone and then, like the tenor sax, up an additional octave to place its entire compass in the treble clef.
21. Many of the new models also possess the low E-flat.

The use of clarinets for an arpeggio accompaniment is dependent upon the flexibility of the bass clarinet for the lowest voice.

In full band scoring the bass clarinet divides its services between reinforcing a counter-melody in the baritone-tenor register, and doubling the bass.

B-FLAT CONTRA-BASS CLARINET

The contra-bass clarinet is a transposing instrument in B-flat and is always written in the treble clef.[22] Its compass is as follows:

The tone of the contra-bass clarinet is reedy with a heavy menacing quality. Its facility is limited and only passages of moderate speed are possible. Barely a few of the largest symphonic bands can boast of this instrument in their ensembles.[23] Its exclusive use is to double the bass or replace that instrument when a low reed bass is desired.

---

22. As the greater part of the compass of this instrument is below the staff, its part (after transposition) is written an additional two octaves higher centrally placing its entire compass in the treble clef.
23. American publications for the band do not include a part for the contra-bass clarinet.

CLARINET SUMMATION

Except for size all clarinets are similar in construction, and identical in fingering. All have a written E below the staff as the lowest note.[24] Knowledge of this similarity and the key of the various clarinets enables us to instantly find the lowest concert note playable on each instrument.

Reference to the chart below will show that with an E as the lowest written note, the E-flat clarinet sounds a minor third higher, i.e., "G." The B-flat clarinet sounds a tone lower than written, i.e., "D," etc. Frequent reference will fix the lowest concert note of each clarinet firmly in mind.

Ex. 50

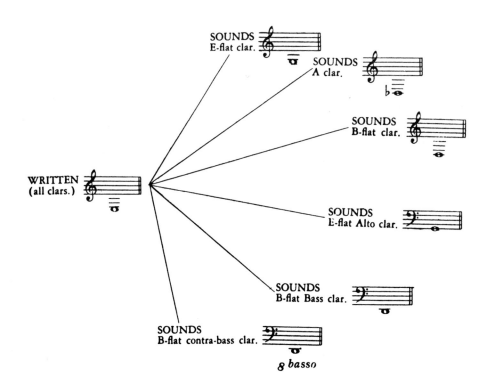

---

24. Some of the late model Bass clarinets have a low E-flat.

SAXOPHONE

The saxophones used in the band are four: E-flat Alto, B-flat Tenor, E-flat Baritone, and B-flat Bass.[25] All are transposing instruments and all are written in the treble clef. The compass of the family is as follows:

Ex. 51

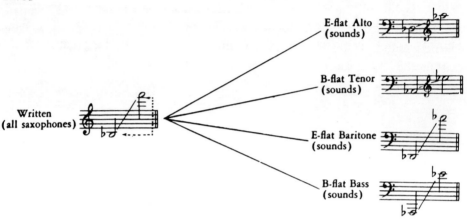

While classed as a reed instrument the tone of the saxophone is actually a combination of brass and reed. These instruments have great value in the band for their ability to blend the tone of the brass instruments with those of the other reed instruments. Singly, and as a group, they blend equally well with either brass or reed. This brassy-reed tonal quality is both strident or mellow as desired. The upper register is harsh and piercing, the middle mellow and sonorous, the lower register is thick, heavy, and of great power. The quality of tone is even throughout the entire compass and all are capable of fast execution.

Due to the insufficient number of alto and bass clarinets in the average band the saxophones are valuable for their ability to assume the functions of these instruments in extending the reed family to the lowest notes of the bass register.

---

25. The soprano saxophone, pitched in B-flat, a fifth above the alto, is not considered in this volume as it is seldom used in band, orchestra, or dance band. This instrument is rapidly becoming obsolete and parts for it are not included in published band material.

E-FLAT ALTO SAXOPHONE

Though seldom used as a solo instrument the brilliant tone and easy facility of this instrument well equip it for this purpose. Solo passages of a lyrical or technical nature are equally effective and colorful, and in the hands of an expert performer, this instrument, as a soloist, can compare favorably with the clarinet or trumpet. Shostakovich, in his Polka from "The Golden Age," has a short passage for alto solo that is very effective.

The greatest value is realized from this instrument when it is used to support a passage for weaker woodwinds to strengthen their tonal quality and volume. In the following example the weak middle register of the clarinets is greatly strengthened by the addition, in unison, of the alto saxophone. The alto assists, but does not impair the clarinet tone, and the resulting blend is an improvement over the clarinets alone.

In like manner, the alto is also used to support a clarinet passage an octave lower to gain the same strengthening effect.

B-FLAT TENOR SAXOPHONE

The tenor saxophone is rarely used for solo passages, its chief function being one of support for other reeds and brass in the tenor register. The warm mellow tone of this instrument, with its easy facility, renders it very valuable for this purpose. In many instances it is used to double the alto saxophone an octave lower.

Adding the tenor saxophone to a solo for baritone horn will mellow and smooth the brass quality of the latter. The combined tonal quality is richer and more lyrical than either instrument alone.

Alto and tenor saxophones in unison are a very strong and rich quality especially with the baritone saxophone an octave lower.

E-FLAT BARITONE SAXOPHONE

Like the tenor saxophone, the baritone is mainly an instrument of support, and is very rarely used for solo passages. The register covered by this instrument is the weakest in the band due to the insufficient numbers of alto, bass clarinets, and bassoons. The baritone saxophone with its full tone and ample volume is ideal to strengthen this register. This facility alone makes it the most valuable of all the saxophones.

The greatest use of the baritone is in supporting low reeds in unison. Passages for bass clarinets and bassoons, when balanced against the full band, are ably supported by the addition of the baritone saxophone. While there is a possibility that the saxophone tone may dominate this mixture, there is no other instrument better equipped to blend with this grouping. In the example below, if the bassoons alone were assigned to the melody, it is doubtful that a proper balance could be achieved between their tone and that of the accompaniment. Adding the baritone saxophone strengthens the melodic line and balances the passage.

Passages for alto and tenor saxophones in unison or octaves, with the baritone supporting the lowest voice, are a rich and strong color.

The baritone in the low register blends very well with the tubas and is often used to double them in the octave above.

B-FLAT BASS SAXOPHONE

The bass saxophone is essentially a bass instrument and being quite large and clumsy, is limited, due to the effort required to play it, to passages of moderate speed and duration.

Very few of even the largest bands can boast of having this instrument in their ensemble,[26] and the lack of interest in this instrument is to be regretted. Despite its ponderous size, lack of facility, and demands on performers, it is a much needed instrument in the band.

The tone is very rich and the volume considerable with a surprising dynamic control. As a substitute for the tuba in full band scoring, when a mellow reed bass is desired, the bass saxophone is unsurpassed.

Its present function in the band is to double the tubas for added strength and to temper their brass tone. Both of these functions are apparent in the use of the instrument as exemplified below.

26. Not all American band publications include a part for this instrument.

SAXOPHONE CHOIR

The usual band score includes a quintette of saxophones: two E-flat Altos, one B-flat Tenor, one E-flat Baritone and one B-flat Bass.[27] It is as a group that the saxophones assert their strongest individuality and render their greatest service to the band.

The ability of this group to blend equally well with brass or reeds, their ease of execution, and fullness of tone, render them capable of performing any required function. In doubling the horns, trombones, and tubas in tutti passages, they contribute their strength of tone and sharpness of attack.

Ex.60

Ex.61

In sustained harmonies for trombones, the addition of saxophones mellows the brass tone of the trombones and assists the legato quality.

Ex.62

Passages for divided clarinets, when doubled by saxophones an octave lower, are given a sweeping rich quality much similar to the effect achieved by the modern dance band.

---

27. The inclusion of the bass saxophone part depends upon the publication and the demands of the composition.

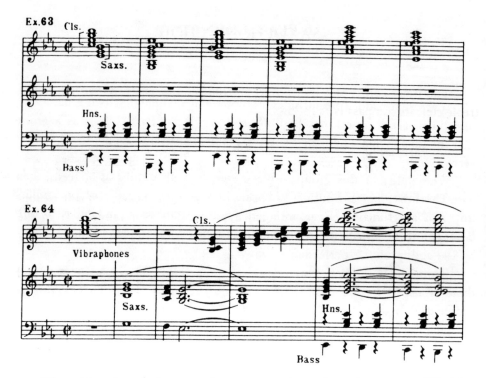

The virtuosity of the saxophone group is perhaps best exemplified by the following extract in which the alto saxophones double the reeds an octave lower, and the tenor and baritone saxophones assist the alto and bass clarinets and bassoons with a running figure.

It is to be hoped that in the future the saxophones in the band will achieve their true position of importance. Their present usage as supporting instruments is very valuable but this function uses only a small portion of their ability. Future consideration of the distinctiveness of this family (not excluding the wonderful bass saxophone) will lead to their use as a separate and distinct reed choir of rare beauty.

B-FLAT CORNET

The B-flat cornet is a transposing instrument and is always written in the treble clef. Its compass is as follows:

The lower notes, up to B-flat below the staff are heavy, difficult to control, and awkward to finger with any rapidity. The best range is from the B-flat below the staff to the A above the staff. The upper register is limited only by the ability of the performer.

Throughout the best range of the instrument all the tones are even and there is no noticeable change of register. In familiar keys the fingering is simple and practicable. The intonation is good and alternate fingerings are available for some notes enabling the performer to make further improvements.

The cornet has a larger bore tubing than the trumpet resulting in a more lyrical and mellow quality of tone. Ease of double and triple tonguing, facilitating rapid scales and arpeggios, has equipped this instrument as capable of great solo virtuosity. Band literature abounds with brilliant technical and melodic passages for the cornet.

In the band the cornet is the leader of the brass family and acts as concertmaster of that group. It is intrusted with the greatest share. of solo brass passages.

The cornet is often used in combination with other instruments, both brass and reed, to strengthen a passage. Doubling the reeds an octave lower is a common usage.

When strengthening horns, trombones or baritones, the cornet plays an octave higher, adding great brilliance to the passage.

Two or three cornets in duet or trio form are an excellent tonal blend.

The brilliant tone and flexibility of the cornet well equip it as the leader of all brass writings. In tutti brass passages it is the highest voice and leading instrument.

The complete brass family is occasionally used to play sustained chords. This type of writing is very effective due to the great dynamic range possessed by these instruments.

Cornets, in soli or in parts, are ideally suited to passages of a military or fanfare character. Their biting precision and brilliant tone quality is often utilized as follows:

The natural tone of the cornet is sometimes altered by the use of mutes.[28] While there are many different kinds of mutes, Shastock, Straight, Cup, Solotone, etc.[29] they all have two main functions. First, all mutes reduce the volume of natural tone; and second, each mute imparts its particular quality of tone.

In a muted passage it is necessary to mark the part correctly so that the player will know what mute to use and when to use it. Immediately preceding a passage to be played muted, the words, Straight mute, or Cup mute (whatever mute is desired) should be written. When the passage is over and it is desired that the player play the next passage without mute the word "open" is written.[30] Ample time is necessary for the player to insert and remove the mute.

Mutes should not be used in the extreme upper or lower register of the instrument. In the low register the mute rattles in the bell of the instrument and spoils the tonal effect. As the mute impedes the passage of air through the horn, muted passages in the extreme upper register place a great strain on the

28. Conical shaped implements of wood or metal inserted in the bell of the instrument.
29. The straight mute is the most commonly used in the band and is carried by all trumpet, cornet, and trombone players. When a passage is simply marked muted, without any particular mute designation, the straight mute is used.
30. The Italian notation, con sordino (with mute) and senza sordino (open) should not be used for brass mutes. These terms are for string mutes and should not be used for any others.

performer. The best register for the most effective use of the mute is as follows:

In solo passages the proper selection of mute will fit the instrument mc closely to the character of the melody, and by diminishing its volume, permit a lighter accompaniment. The following passage from "Salute To The Allies" illustrates this usage. Three solo cornets in Cup mutes preserve the religious mood in answering the oboe. Open cornets would be wholly out of character, both in volume and quality of tone.

Short, rhythmic chords for muted trumpets, cornets and trombones are especially effective as the mute imparts a quality of crispness and incisiveness to the tone.

Mutes are frequently used in South American and Spanish music for character of tone. If the brass were open in the following passage their volume would be out of proportion with the clarinet melody and the tonal quality would not be in character.

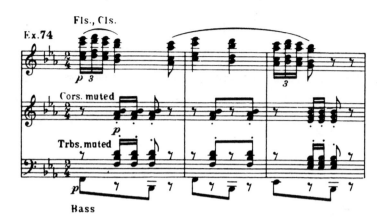

Proper use of the contrast between open and muted passages is a startling effect. In the "American Salute" passage below, the melody is stated, first, by cornet and trombone (open) in octaves. A few bars later the melody is presented by the same instruments, this time muted.

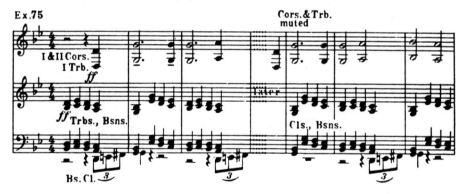

B-FLAT TRUMPET

The B-flat trumpet is a transposing instrument and is always written in the treble clef. Its compass is the same as the cornet.

The trumpet is an exact replica of the cornet in construction except that the bore (tubing) is slightly smaller and the instrument longer.

All technical material used to describe the cornet, including the use of mutes, applies to the trumpet.

Due to its smaller bore the trumpet possesses a more brilliant and piercing quality of tone than the cornet. In the band the trumpet is subordinate to the cornet and is chiefly used for fanfares and martial passages where its brassy brilliance of tone is desired. The following passages, scored for trumpets, would have less fire and brilliance if scored for cornets.

The smaller bore of this instrument results in a thinner tone, and this quality, especially when muted, is light and delicate. The following example illustrates the use of this quality of tone as an echo effect.

Ex.78

Unison writing for cornets and trumpets in fortissimo passages is very effective, the combined tone quality benefiting from the brassy brilliance of the trumpet.

Ex.79

Ex.80

Trumpets are also used to double cornets in fortissimo passages when the cornets are written in duet or trio form.

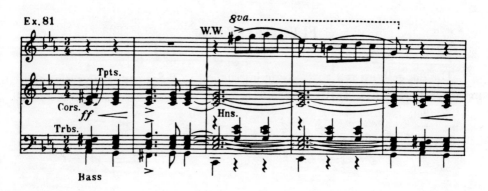

FLEUGELHORN

The fleugelhorn is a transposing instrument in B-flat and is always written in the treble clef. Its compass is as follows: [31]

WRITTEN    SOUNDS

The fleugelhorn is similar to the cornet in construction except that the bore (tubing) and bell is much larger and the instrument longer and heavier. All technical material used to describe the cornet applies to the fleugelhorn.[32]

Actually an alto cornet, the fleugelhorn has a very warm resonant tone, similar to the baritone and alto. It is exclusively used in the lower part of its compass as a solo instrument and to function as a 3rd cornet.

While still listed in the bands' instrumentation, the fleugelhorn, along with the E-flat clarinet, is very seldom used and is rapidly becoming extinct.[33]

---

31. Like the other brass instruments, the upper limits of the compass are limited only by the ability of the performer.
32. Except mutes, which are not used with fleugelhorns.
33. Only occasional band publications include a part for this instrument.

FRENCH HORN

The French horn is a transposing instrument in F[34] and is always written in the treble clef.[35] Its compass is as follows:

WRITTEN   SOUNDS

Throughout the compass of the horn all the notes are even and there is no noticeable change of register.

Except for solo passages the extreme high and low registers of the horn compass are to be avoided. The lowest notes are difficult and uncertain of intonation. The high notes, while very brilliant, (similar to a trumpet) are hazardous for the performer. For general band writing it is well to stay within the suggested practical register.

The tone quality of the horn is one of heroic, majestic beauty. The low register is warm and resonant, admirable for melodies of moderate movement and sustained tones. The middle register has a brassier quality of tone and it is in this register that the horn is most frequently used. The upper register is very strong and has great powers of penetration. This register should be used sparingly, and only when the horn is to dominate.

The ability of the horn to blend with the woodwinds has caused it to be sometimes classified as a woodwind instrument.[36] While this classification is doubtful, due to its brass construction, it is true that the horn blends better with the woodwinds than any other instrument of brass.[37]

The beautiful and majestic tone quality of the horn is covered in the band by the superior numbers of other brasses. It is further subordinated by employing it, chiefly, as a rhythm instrument. While this is an important function of the horn it is hardly flattering to its tremendous ability and tonal beauty.

---

34. Early symphonic works have horn parts in all keys, E-flat, G, D, C, etc. When these works were written the horn had no valves and could play in only one key at a time. With this instrument only the notes of the harmonic series were possible, like the bugle. Key changes were affected by the insertion of "crooks" (pieces of tubing) into the instrument. The present-day horn has valves and is a fully chromatic instrument throughout its compass. For this reason it is perfectly proper to write a key signature for the horn, treating it like all other transposing instruments.
35. Composers have used all manner of notations in writing for horns. All these practices are to be avoided. The horn should be written in the treble clef as a transposing instrument in F.
36. The horn is included in the instrumentation of the woodwind quintet with the flute, oboe, clarinet, and bassoon.
37. Excepting the saxophones.

The necessity of strong rhythm in some types of band scoring, particularly marches, has resulted in the horns being assigned to this function. In two, three, or four parts, they carry the harmonic basis in a rhythmic fashion. For this function it is best to keep the horns in the middle register where the greatest control of dynamics is possible.

The above combination of horns and bass forms a solid rhythmic and harmonic foundation and is similar to the function of the piano in a dance band. It is not always necessary or desirable to have four parts for horns, in which case one or more of the notes are doubled.

Not always certain that there are four horns, it is a common practice to write the best interval of the chord for the first and second horns and then complete the chord with the third and fourth horns. This practice frequently results in the third horn being above the second horn. For example, the following rhythmic passage for horns would be assigned as indicated:

Ex.85

Inasmuch as this practice does not disturb the balance of tone it is an excellent example of practical writing. Furthermore, when two horns are written on one part, it results in wider intervals, and greater ease of reading.[38]

Horns, with their close blend of tones and dynamic control are excellent for sustained harmonies.

Ex.86

Solo passages for horns in unison are heroic and dramatic.

Ex.87

Passages in three octaves for horns, tromboñes, and basses have great power and vitality.

---

38. In published band material it is customary to have separate parts for the first and second horns. The third and fourth are usually written on one part.

Horns in two or more parts have a heavy driving quality as expressed in the following example:

Horns have two methods of muting their tone. The preferred method is done with the hand in the bell stopping the flow of air. This diminishes the volume and veils the tone. It is indicated by a small cross (+) over the notes desired muted. Horns also possess a mute which is inserted into the bell of the instrument. It is similar in tone color to the straight mute of the trumpet and trombone. Like these instruments, it is indicated in the same fashion, and time must be allowed for its insertion and removal.

E-FLAT ALTO (MELLOPHONE)

The alto is a transposing instrument in E-flat and is always written in the treble clef. Its compass is as follows:

This instrument is very similar in construction to the French horn and has pistons instead of rotary valves. The pistons are played with the fingers of the right hand and the bell held with the left, the exact opposite of the French horn.

The alto (mellophone) is solely a band instrument and is a substitute for the French horn. The fingering is very similar to that of the trumpet and any trumpet player can quickly adapt himself to this instrument.

The tone of the alto is not a good duplicate of the horn and has none of its beauty. However, since the French horn is a difficult instrument to master, and the alto is not, it is a very practicable substitute. Publishers of band music recognize the necessity of this substitution and include in their publications horn parts in E-flat for the altos. With the exception of the key these are exact duplicates of the horn parts.

As this instrument is a substitute for the horn its band function is exactly the same. All material pertaining to the use of the horn is applicable to the alto.

The alto, like the horn, can be muted by placing the hand in the bell. However, a mechanical mute is rarely employed.

TROMBONE (TENOR)

The trombone is a concert instrument and is written in both the bass and tenor clef.[39] Its compass is as follows·

The proficiency of modern trombonists has greatly extended the upper register of the instrument. Passages up to E-flat, F, and G are a common occurrence. However, for general writing, it is advisable to limit the range to the B-flat indicated.

The tone of the trombone is broad and majestic. The lower tones are menacing and foreboding while those of the upper register are light and lyrical, similar to the horn quality.

As the trombone is played by moving a slide, care must be taken not to write fast passages in the lower register. Rapid changing of slide positions in this register is difficult and sometimes impossible to execute. Below is a chart of the slide positions of the trombone.

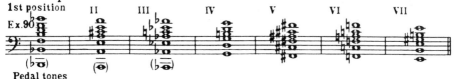

Reference to this chart will show that the lowest B-flat is in the first position (nearest the performer) and the lowest F is in the sixth position (at arms length). Rapid playing of these notes is almost impossible. However, if the F were up an octave both notes are then in the same slide position and execution is simple. Similarly a scale from the lowest B-flat is very difficult to play with any rapidity as the first two notes, B-flat and C are in the first and sixth positions respectively.

Further reference to the position chart will show that above the E all notes are obtainable in two or more positions on the instrument. This enables the performer to select the position that will best facilitate his playing.

The trombone ranks with the cornet in executing solo passages. The facility and brilliant tone of this instrument equip it as capable of great virtuosity. Melodic or technical passages are performed equally well and are very effective.

---

39. Passages in the extreme upper register are usually written in the tenor clef. The use of this clef minimizes the number of ledger lines making the part easier to read.

Fortissimo passages for trombones in unison are a magnificent, majestic declaration.

Close blending of two or three trombones can be both militant or suave as desired. The power of the following extract,

can be compared with the next tender, lyrical quotation.

In combination with the basses, the trombones add tremendous power and breadth of tone.

Ex.95

Trombones are often used to double the cornets an octave lower. This type of brass writing has great powers of penetration.

Ex.96

Sustained harmonies for trombones have a rich and noble quality of tone. For this type of scoring, trombones are occasionally used in preference to horns because of their greater volume of tone and lower register.

Ex.97

Similarly, rhythmic passages, usually assigned to horns, are frequently played by the trombones, especially when the horns are otherwise occupied or a greater volume of tone is desired.

In the passage below the melody is scored for the horns, and the trombones are assigned to a rhythmic background.

Trombones are preferred to horns in the next example because of their heavier quality of tone.

Like the cornet and trumpet, the tone of the trombone may be altered by the use of mutes. The same types of mutes are used and the directions for their use are similar. Furthermore, like the other brass instruments, time must be allowed for the insertion and removal of the mutes and the extreme upper and lower registers are to be avoided when using them.

BASS TROMBONE

The bass trombone is a concert instrument and is always written in the bass clef. Its compass is as follows:

The bass trombone is seldom honored by a special part in the band[40] and when present in the ensemble is usually considered to be the 3rd trombone. Due to its larger bore and bell it is well fitted for this use as it sounds the low register better than the tenor trombone. Because of this assignment its extended compass is seldom used and it is considered to have an "E" bottom like the tenor trombone.

All references to the tenor trombone are applicable to the bass trombone.

---

40. Not all band publications include a part for bass trombone.

BARITONE (EUPHONIUM)

The baritone is a concert[41] instrument and is always written in the bass clef.[42] Its compass is as follows:

WRITTEN    SOUNDS

Chiefly a band instrument, the baritone has great agility and many functions. The tone is mellow, full, and even throughout the entire compass. The fingering is simple and facile and the instrument is very expressive in melodic and countermelodic passages.

Gay, bright, melodies are a happy assignment for the baritone and the following example illustrates its robust charm.

The baritone, with its flexibility and dynamic control, is equally well suited to passages of a lyrical nature.

41. The baritone is often written in the treble clef a transposing instrument in B-flat, an octave and a tone above its actual pitch, similar to the tenor saxophone. With this notation the fingering of the instrument is similar to that of the cornet, enabling performers to transfer from one instrument to the other. Publishers of band music recognize this practicability and include two baritone parts in each arrangement; one in the bass clef as a concert instrument, and another in the treble clef as a B-flat instrument.
42. Like the trombone, though less frequently, the tenor clef is used for baritone to minimize the use of ledger lines.

Ex.102 Bar. Saxs.

In construction the baritone is actually a small bore B-flat bass and bears the same relationship to the tuba as the cello to the string bass. The baritone and tuba, both valved instruments, and equally facile, are an ideal combination for the performance of octave bass passages.

Ex.103 W.W.

Ex.104

Ex.105

In unison with trombones, the baritones add breadth of tone, and the resultant combination is slightly mellower in timbre.

Ex.106 Low WW., Saxs., Hns.

Saxophones and low clarinets, when supported by baritones, (in unison or the octave) have a bigger and fuller quality of tone.

Ex.107 Fls., Piccs., *8va*

Ex.108 Cls., Alto Sax.

The baritone is often used to reinforce the cornet an octave lower. This scoring is very fluid and expressive due to the close affinity of these instruments. In full band scoring the baritone is used to either support the cornet in the lower octave, or double the tuba in the upper octave.

The instrumentation of the average band usually includes more baritones than are necessary. When scoring passages of delicate balance it is advisable to indicate the exact number of baritones desired.

TUBAS

The band uses tubas in E-flat and BB-flat.[43] In spite of the keys in which they are constructed they are written as concert instruments in the bass clef. Their compasses are as follows:

The tubas are the foundation of the brass family and the bass of the band. Both E-flat and BB-flat tubas have considerable facility and the tone is even throughout. In band scoring, one part, marked basses, is written for both E-flat and BB-flat instruments. This part is sometimes written in octaves to keep the E-flat tuba within its compass. It is not necessary to mark this distribution as it is generally understood that the upper voice is for the E-flat tuba and the lower for the BB-flat.

Sounding a rhythmic bass is the most common function of the tubas in the band. These instruments speak easily and have good dynamic control. The following example illustrates the basses scored in unison as the part is well within the compasses of both E-flat and BB-flat instruments.

Ex.109

A little later the part is written in octaves as the lower voice is beyond the compass of the E-flat tuba.

---

43. Some BB-flat (double B-flat) tubas have a fourth valve which extends their compass down to B-flat. This extended register is seldom used and all brass basses are considered as having an "E" as their lowest note.
44. The E-flat tuba is a smaller and lighter instrument more practical for marching bands.

Ex.110

Tubas are very powerful instruments and in the interest of appearance some bands have many more of these instruments than are necessary to balance the ensemble. In passages where the balance is critical it is advisable to indicate the amount of bass desired by notating one only, two only, etc.

Ex.111

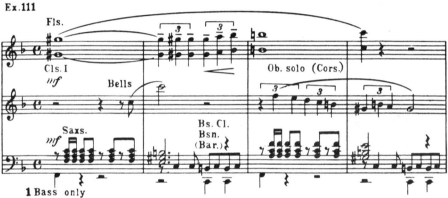

In the above example the bass is written for a solo tuba and the accompaniment for three saxophones. A little later (Ex. 112) all the basses are desired and the accompaniment is balanced by adding horns and indicating all clarinets.

Ex.112

Due to their extreme low register the tubas are seldom reinforced in unison, except by the low reeds. When it is desired to strengthen the bass, the octave above is used for reinforcement assigned to baritones and trombones.

Ex. 113

BRASS SUMMATION

The extreme low note of each instrument is a practical rule-of-thumb for a beginning familiarity with its compass. In previous summations it was indicated that for clarinets the note is a Concert "D." For saxophones the lowest note is a written B-flat. For the brass family, excepting the horns, E-flat tuba, and bass trombone, a Concert "E" is the basis.

Ex. 114

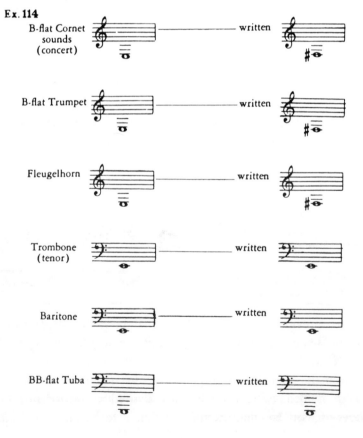

PERCUSSION

Percussion instruments are divided into two general classes: instruments of definite pitch, and instruments of indefinite pitch. We will consider the instruments of indefinite pitch first as they include the snare drum and bass drum, the basis of the percussion section of the band.

SNARE DRUM — BASS DRUM

These instruments are never tuned to a definite pitch but are tuned for tone and response by increasing or decreasing the tension on the head (skin). While these instruments are occasionally used separately, they are usually regarded as a team and are written together on the bass staff as follows:

Ex.115

The use of the bass staff with the snare drum on the "E" space and the bass drum on the "A" space has no significance except custom. However, this notation is universal.

Working as a team, the snare drum and bass drum support the basic rhythmic elements of a passage. The snare drum supports the alto-tenor rhythmic elements, (horns, trombones, etc.) and the bass drum supports the bass line (tubas, etc.). As exemplified below, this is the most common scoring for these instruments and their greatest contribution to the band.

Ex.116

As stated previously, each instrument may be used independently to support or emphasize any rhythmic or dynamic element in the score. Both are capable of a "roll" which is the percussion equivalent of a sustained tone. The snares on the snare drums may be released from contact with the head to produce a muffled, hollow sound. This is indicated on the part by "snares on," "snares off" or "muffled drum."

Ex. 117

Ex. 118

TOM-TOMS

A native, tribal type of drum, usually in sets of two or more, and similar in tone to the muffled snare drum. For a variety of effects they are played with fingers, soft mallets, or drum sticks. These drums are used chiefly for Oriental, Indian, and tribal color and rhythm. They are notated on the bass staff, along with, or in place of, the snare drum.

TAMBOURINES — CASTANETS

These well-known Spanish and South American implements are used chiefly when their distinctive coloring is desired. The tambourine is usually laid on the snare drum and played with drum sticks. Modern castanets are mounted on a board with a handle greatly simplifying their execution. The tambourines and castanets are usually scored and notated together on a separate part. A single line is used on which to write their rhythms.

Ex.119 With spirit

MARRACAS — CLAVES

These South American instruments of wonderful rhythmic color are often used in the band. Their system of notation is the same as used for tambourines and castanets.

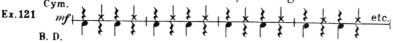

Marracas Ex.120
Claves

GONGS — CYMBALS — TRIANGLE

These effects are usually notated by diamond shaped quarter, half, and whole notes (or simple crosses) to give some indication of their duration. When a gong or cymbal tone of short duration is desired the word "choked" is used indicating that the performer is to stop the vibration with his hand. When a long tone is desired it is indicated by "let ring."

Ex.121 Cym. / B. D.

Ex.122

TRAPS

Implements as whistles, cow bells, wood blocks, sleigh bells, etc., are indicated by name on the drum part using diamond or cross shaped notes for rhythm and duration.

Ex.123 Bright tempo

Ex.124

Sandpaper blocks or brushes on S. D.

INSTRUMENTS OF DEFINITE PITCH

TIMPANI

Timpani are usually present in sets of two, three, or four, (usually two for bands) and are concert instruments written in the bass clef. The compasses of the most common large and small timpani are as follows:

Except for special effects, the timpani are always tuned to the dominant and tonic of the prevailing key. Modern timpani are equipped with pedals simplifying change of pitch and experienced performers are extremely efficient with these controls, even executing scales and melodies. However, this facility is above the average performer and it is advised that he be given time to change pitch. The pitches are indicated above the part and the part is written on the proper lines and spaces but without accidentals and key signatures.

Ex.125 Db & Ab

The timpani have a very resonant, mellow tone and are frequently scored for solos. The roll is very smooth and even, and used crescendo and diminuendo, it is a splendid effect.

Ex.126

CHIMES

The standard set of tubular chimes is a rack of eighteen chromatic notes which has a compass as follows:

WRITTEN
and
SOUNDS

The chimes are played by striking with a rawhide headed mallet. A damper, operated by the foot, controls the duration of tone. Rapid passages are unsuited for chimes as their long vibrations and resonance have a tendency to prolong one note into the next.

Ex.127

Ex.128

BELLS: GLOCKENSPIEL — LYRE

These instruments are identical except for mounting. The glockenspiel are mounted in a case and played horizontal. The lyre bells are set in a lyre shaped frame and with the help of a leather harness are carried by a marching performer and played in a vertical position. The compass of both instruments is identical:

WRITTEN and SOUND

Bells have a shorter wave length and less resonance than chimes and are capable of reasonably rapid passages.

Ex.129

Ex.130

XYLOPHONE — MARIMBA

The marimba differs from the xylophone only in that it has a lower register, a more mellow tone, and is usually played with soft mallets. For warm, resonant effects with two, three, or four mallets, the marimba is the proper choice. Its compass is as follows:

WRITTEN and SOUNDS

Ex.131

The xylophone is usually played with hard, or semi-hard mallets, and has a dry, brittle tone. It is capable of rapid scales, glissandos, tremolos, and is a very effective solo instrument. Its compass is as follows:

WRITTEN
and
SOUNDS

In the band the xylophone is used to reinforce and add its color to the high woodwind and muted brasses. The resultant combination has a sharper and more pungent sound plus a more definite attack.

INSTRUMENTS OCCASIONALLY USED IN THE BAND

HARP

The harp is a concert instrument and its music is written on the great staff (like the piano) Its compass is as follows:

Arpeggios, chords, glissandos, and harmonics are the most characteristic passages for the harp. Except as a solo instrument, the harp is seldom used in the band.

CELLO

The cello is a concert instrument and its music is written in the bass and tenor clef. Its strings and compass are as follows:

Except for a few experiments to support or replace baritones and euphoniums, the cello is rarely used in the band.

CELESTE

The celeste is a concert instrument and its music is always written in the bass and treble clef. Its compass is as follows:

The celeste is used like the harp for broken chords and faint melodies. It has very little volume of tone and for that reason composers and arrangers of band music prefer the glockenspiel.

STRING BASS

The string bass is a concert instrument and its music is always written in the bass clef. Its strings and compass are as follows:

In recent years the string bass has become a very popular, and almost standard, member of the band. As this instrument sounds an octave lower than written, a separate part is written for it. Played with the bow (arco) or plucked with the fingers (pizz) it has a warm full tone and good facility. The string bass is used in the band to color and soften the brass bass, for solo passages (usually pizzicato, Ex. 134), and to support the reed bass (bsns., bass clar., etc.).

Ex.134

45. Stg. Bass (pizz.)

Part Two
INSTRUMENTAL VOICES

INSTRUMENTAL VOICES

In the previous chapter on instrumentation each instrument of the band was discussed as an individual. All the possibilities, limitations, tonal colors and characteristics peculiar to each instrument were noted and charted. **WP 1**

However, since arranging is the art of combining instruments, to progress in the study of scoring for band it is also necessary to view each instrument in its perspective as a member of the band. No longer is an instrument an entity in itself but a contributing member of a group. Individuality is now subordinate to the more important function of membership. Each instrument brings its own personality to the ensemble and the sum total of these personalities is the complex musical instrument known as the band.

With scoring in mind, the first impression of a band in person or on score paper, is one of bewilderment. There are so many instruments of different sizes, shapes, and construction that it is a case of not being able to see the band because of the instruments.

In order not to be confused a clearer look at the basic structure of the band is imperative. We know from our study of the chapter on instrumentation that all instruments can be divided into general families of timbre: brass, reed, double reed, and percussion. **WP 2**

While this division is important and does much to clarify the initial impression of confusion it is a division of tonal color and not of functions. In studying these four classifications it is apparent that each family has many members and each member has different characteristics and functions than its nearest relative. A further division is necessary; one that will, in a general way, define the function of each instrument in the ensemble of the band.

QUARTET WRITING

A basic approach to scoring for the band can best be begun by a brief consideration of the human voice. All human voices are divided into four types, or registers, namely: soprano, alto, tenor, and bass. As the human voice was probably the first musical instrument, all mechanical instruments were originally constructed in imitation of these vocal registers. The fundamental compass of each of the vocal registers is as follows:

Ex. 135

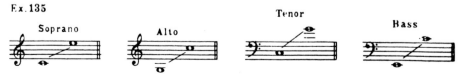

All musical instruments can be fundamentally designated as soprano, alto, tenor, or bass in that the general playing compass of each represents one of the above vocal registers. The fact that the compass of an instrument exceeds its vocal register by having more tones above or below, does not alter its classification. When one of the vocal registers falls within the best playing compass of an instrument, the instrument is designated by the name of that vocal register.

Compare the compass of the alto saxophone with the register of the alto voice. While the instrument has tones to spare above and below the alto voice register, these are the extremes of its compass and its best playing area is in the alto voice register. Further, compare the compasses of the trombone (originally termed tenor trombone) and the tenor saxophone with the tenor voice register. It is also apparent that the flute and oboe, while not generally designated as soprano instruments, have the greatest portion of their compass in that voice register. Other instruments, for example the clarinet, are not so easily classified. The clarinet compass covers the soprano, alto, and almost all of the tenor voice registers. This latter register can be disregarded for classification purposes as it includes the extreme low tones of the clarinet compass. The clarinet is actually both an alto and soprano instrument and is utilized in both registers. This classification is further complicated by the mis-naming of the "alto" clarinet, which is actually a tenor instrument as comparison of its compass and register will show. The clarinet family as a quartet, is more actually composed of the B-flat clarinet as both a soprano and alto instrument, the alto clarinet as a tenor instrument, with the bass clarinet completing the quartet.[2]

It is now possible to divide all the instruments of the band into four REGISTER classifications. (Ex. 136) **WP 3**

This classification is the most pertinent in that it is a fundamental approach and practical guide to all instrumental scoring. All instruments must first be recognized as representing a portion of the great staff. Within the scope of a specific number of lines and spaces each instrument has a facility that awaits the arranger. The timbre of each instrument is of secondary consideration. Given a melody for instrumental scoring, the first consideration is to its register. Where does it lie in the staff, and what instruments are available? When the instruments in that register are ascertained, selection is merely a matter of the quality or quantity of tone desired; reed, double reed, or brass? Except for a special effect, and even then only sparingly, is it advisable to score an instrument in the extremes of its compass. Good scoring demands that every instrument have all the notes of its part within its practical playing compass. Use of the extremes of the compass of any instrument is risky, and in most cases, unnecessary. **WP 4**

2. Similar to the string quartet where one violin is the soprano instrument and the other is an alto instrument, with the viola and cello as tenor and bass respectively. Like the alto clarinet, the viola, (originally named alto) is actually a tenor instrument.

INSTRUMENTAL VOICES

Ex. 136

INSTRUMENT	SOPRANO[1]	ALTO	TENOR	BASS
Piccolo (C and D-flat)	A			
Flute	A			
Alto Flute	B	A		
Oboe	A			
English Horn	B	A		
E-flat Clarinet	A	B		
B-flat Clarinet	A	B	C	
E-flat Alto Clarinet		B	A	C
B-flat Bass Clarinet		C	B	A
B-flat Contra Bass Clarinet			B	A
Bassoon		C	B	A
Contra Bassoon				A
E-flat Alto Saxophone	B	A	C	
B-flat Tenor Saxophone		B	A	C
E-flat Baritone Saxophone			B	A
B-flat Bass Saxophone				A
Cornet (E-flat)	A			
Cornet (B-flat)	A	B		
Trumpet	A	B		
Fleugelhorn	B	A		
French Horn		A	B	
Alto Horn (Mellophone)		A	B	
Trombone		C	A	B
Bass Trombone			B	A
Baritone		C	A	B
Euphonium		C	A	B
E-flat Tuba				A
Tuba (B-flat)				A
Marimba	B	A		
Xylophone	A	B		
Chimes		A		
Steel Bells	A			
Tympani				A

1. The best practical playing register is indicated in the vocal register columns as "A." The next best by "B," etc.

A more complete understanding of the register of instruments can be attained by further study of Ex. 136. Notice that all families of instruments have members in each of the vocal registers. There are soprano, alto, tenor, and bass brass instruments; reed instruments; and double reed instruments. For example, the entire range of the great staff is covered by the combined compasses of the alto, tenor and baritone saxophones.

If a quartet of saxophones is assembled using two alto saxophones as soprano and alto voices, and a tenor and baritone as tenor and bass voices, we can begin simple exercises in scoring.

In Ex. 138 a Bach choral is presented in its original form and then scored for the above suggested quartet of saxophones.

The above is just a simple saxophone scoring of the voices of the choral. Each voice in the choral is assigned to an instrument. This form of writing instruments above one another in accordance with their register, each with its proper clef and key signature, is called a score.

Scored for brass using two B-flat cornets as soprano and alto voices, and a trombone and baritone as tenor and bass voices, the score would be as follows:

Ex 139

For clarinets and double reeds the procedure is exactly the same and their respective scores are exhibited below.

Ex.140

Ex.141

It is apparent that the instrumental assignments in the preceding scores are only a few of many possible combinations. In the saxophone score, reference to the instrumental voices chart (Ex. 136) will show that a tenor saxophone has adequate compass to be assigned to the alto voice and even the bass voice. Even another alto saxophone could be assigned to the tenor voice.

In the brass score a French horn (or mellophone) could be assigned to the alto or tenor voice; or a trombone could be assigned to the alto or bass voice. Similarly in the clarinet and double reed scores many other combinations of instruments are possible.

To reiterate what has been said before, the first consideration of scoring is the selection of the instruments capable, by virtue of compass, to be assigned a specific voice. When this group has been selected, final assignment is dictated first, by the instruments available, and second, the quality and quantity of tone desired. **WP 5**

As this type of writing is the basis of all scoring, numerous examples should be executed by assembling different instrumental quartet combinations other than those suggested. All song books, hymnals, and folk song collections written in quartet style contain excellent material. These exercises will do much to help develop a familiarity with each instrument, its registers, and transposition. For the present use only members of one family for your combinations, all reeds, or all brass.

This procedure, while offered only as a step in the progress of scoring for band, has in itself, great practical value. For the instrumental teacher or performer, it is a simple method of preparing special material for group or class instruction. Transposition of examples will teach and develop facility in different keys and on different registers of each instrument. The supervisor or band leader can use this type of scoring to create solo quartet groups for concerts as well as preparing topical and patriotic material for special functions.

WP 6-7-8

Ex.142

It can readily be seen that all these studies combined form a simple method of scoring for full band. By referring to the instrumental voices chart Ex. 136 it will be seen that it is possible to score the choral (Ex. 142) for full band simply by assigning all the soprano instruments to the soprano voice, the alto instruments to the alto voice, etc. Ex. 143.

It is admitted that this is a very crude method of scoring for band, and serves only as a means of acquainting the student, as early as possible, with scoring for the instruments of the full band. However, with slight modifications, this method would be very practical (and is used) for certain types of material.

Choral Ex. 142 is also the subject of WP 5.

Ex. 143 is an execution of the assignment as proposed. The choral (Ex. 142) is scored for full band by assigning all the Soprano instruments to the Soprano voice, all the Alto instruments to the Alto voice, etc. Notice that some of the Soprano instruments, piccs., flutes, and E-flat clar., are in the lowest part of their compass. These instruments, if written an octave higher, would be in a more comfortable part of their playing range. This would make the melody more predominant and brilliant, as well as eliminating some of the unison duplications.

It will be further noticed that the most numerous instruments of the band (clarinets and cornets) are scored in unison on the Soprano voice. Such a large body of instruments sounding this single voice would make it dominate to an extent that it would greatly overshadow the other three voices. We know from the register chart (Ex. 136) that the clarinets and cornets are effective in the Alto as well as the Soprano register. If we divide these instruments between both of these voices we will affect a better balance of voices and again lessen some of the unison duplications. Similar treatment of the horns by dividing them on the alto and tenor voices and the trombones on the tenor and bass voices will greatly help in balancing these inner voices. When the instruments are in fours, as the horns, the division will be equal. When the instruments are in threes, as the trombones, clarinets, and cornets, score the first and second on the upper voice and the third on the lower voice.

Consideration of the bass will complete our modification. If we refer to the compass of the bass-tuba in the chapter on instrumentation it is apparent that the bass voice of the choral is in the extreme upper compass of that instrument. Writing this instrument an octave lower would bring it in a more comfortable part of its range and provide a firmer bass to the choral.

Ex. 144 is a full page scoring of the same choral (Ex. 142) incorporating the above suggested modifications. Notice that the choral has not been changed, nor have any voices been added or eliminated. Rather, a re-assignment of instruments has been affected with a view of dividing the strength of some instruments for better balance, as well as writing some instruments an octave lower (or higher) to place them in a better playing range. It is obvious on paper, and would be proved by performance, that this is a vast improvement of Ex. 143. Many unison duplications have been eliminated and others dispersed, thus greatly improving the tonal quality of the band. The original range of the choral has been exceeded by two octaves, one below (bass, etc.) and one above (fls., etc.), thus broadening the scope of the band resulting in a fuller and bigger sound. Further modifications may be made in this type of scoring by other assignments of instruments or by omission of instruments. **WP 9**

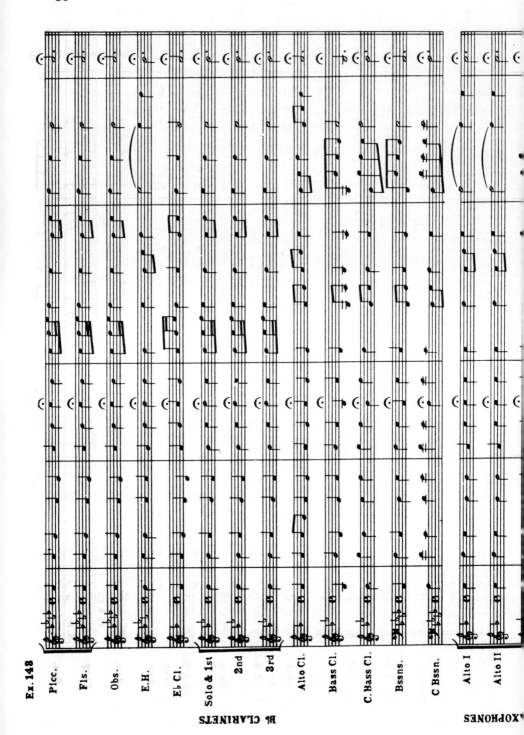

Ex. 148

Picc.
Fls.
Obs.
E.H.
Eb Cl.
Solo & 1st
2nd
3rd
Alto Cl.
Bass Cl.
C. Bass Cl.
Bssns.
C Bssn.
Alto I
Alto II

Bb CLARINETS

XOPHONES

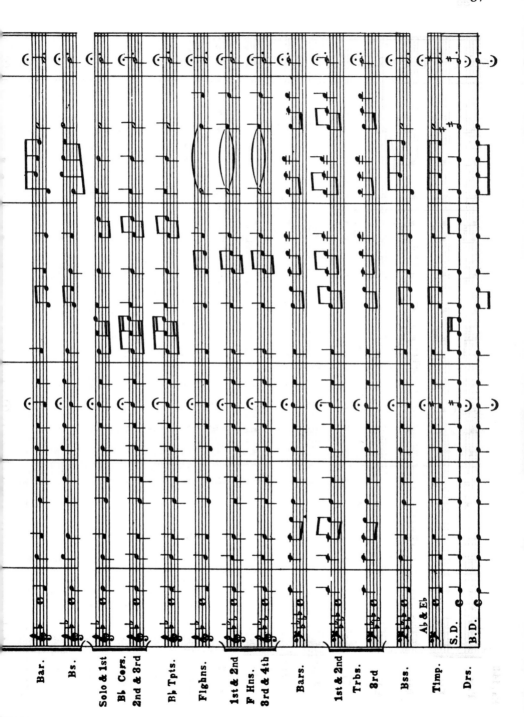

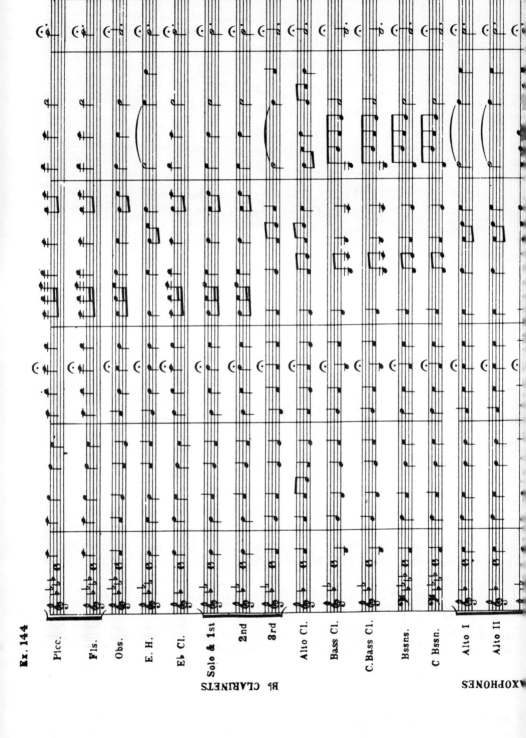

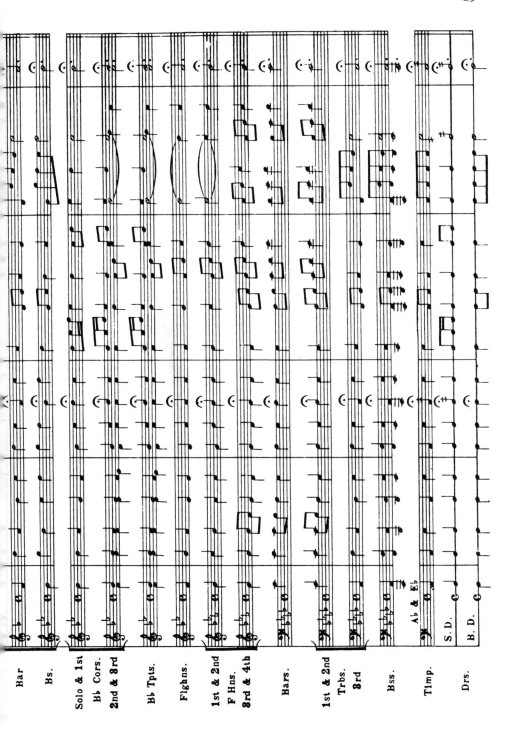

Quartet scoring for band, with these, and other modifications, has great practical value and is commonly used. **WP 10--11- 12**

Ex.145

Ex.146

DIVISION OF VOICES

It has been demonstrated that quartet writing is the method of scoring all the vocal registers, Soprano, Alto, Tenor, and Bass for four or more different musical instruments in open position.[3]

Examination of Ex. 144 will show that while only four voices are scored this arrangement could be played by bands varying from thirty to one hundred or more performers. This is accomplished by many instruments playing in unison and is called unison duplication. Offered as a step in the study of band scoring, and having in itself, great practical value, it is apparent that this method is merely a point of progression. It has accomplished its purpose in demonstrating the general placement of all the instruments of the band, register relations to each other, as well as familiarity with the full band score page.

However, it is quite obvious that band arrangements cannot be written in quartet style throughout with all the instruments playing all the time. This would be a sheer waste of instruments in not taking advantage of the countless tone colors of the band, as well as being monotonous and uninspiring.

It is necessary to create more than four vocal voices to accommodate the many instruments of the band and avoid the many unison duplications. This can be accomplished by a division of voices.

Each of the voices we have used so far, Soprano, Alto, Tenor, and Bass, may be divided into two, three, or even four, parts. In band scoring the division of a voice into three parts is the most commonly used. Reference to Ex. 144 will show that the most numerous instruments of the band, viz: clarinets, cornets, and trombones, are written in three parts; clarinets 1, 2, and 3, cornets 1, 2, and 3, and trombones 1, 2, and 3. This three part writing is in closed position[3] in that the outer voices are never more than an octave apart. As long as the three parts are in closed position and within the confines of an octave they can be termed a division of one voice. If the parts for the first, second, and third cornets are written in closed position they will all be soprano voices in that they are a three part division of the soprano voice. Should the third cornet part be more than an octave away from the first cornet it would be normally trespassing into the alto register and would be termed an alto voice. Similarly used the trombones 1, 2, and 3 would be either tenor or bass

3. Open harmony (position) in four-part writing spreads the three highest voices beyond the compass of an octave.

Closed harmony keeps these three voices within the compass of an octave.

instruments depending upon where the passage lies in the staff. Clarinets 1, 2, and 3 would be either soprano or alto instruments. This procedure does not triple the available voices but does offer an effective method of creating sufficient voices for instrumental scoring, and in such a manner, that unison duplications are avoided.

This three part division of a voice is obtained directly from quartet material. Ex. 147 is a few bars from the original piano part of "El Relicario."

Ex.147

This is a simple example of quartet writing and would serve as an exercise for quartet scoring along with the hymn and folk song material recommended. However, if the voices are compressed to closed position we have an entirely ifferent example. **WP 13**

Ex.148

It can readily be seen that the above distribution is much more practical for instrumental scoring. Instead of a soprano, alto, tenor, and bass voice, we have now, three soprano voices and a bass. No voices have been added or subtracted, the sole change being one of position in that the original tenor voice now occupies a position between the soprano and alto. The three upper voices, being in the soprano register, and in closed position, can be termed a three part division of the soprano voice. They could be assigned to cornets 1, 2, and 3 and the bass voice to the tubas. By doubling the three upper voices an octave lower we can accommodate the three trombones.

Ex.149 Cors. I, II, III

Examination of Ex. 149 will show that the bass voice is in the extreme upper register of the bass compass. This would be an excellent voice for the baritone and the bass would be in a comfortable register if he were to play this voice an octave lower. Writing the basses and baritones in octaves is sound practice and is similar to the orchestral technique of using the cello and bass in octaves. In Ex. 150 the cornets and trombones remain as they were, the original bass voice is assigned to the baritone and the bass doubles this an octave lower. **WP 14**

Ex.150

We will continue this scoring by adding the horns, the last members of the brass family, in the alto and tenor register. Remembering that it is always practical to score fundamentally for the 1st and 2nd horns[4] (then adding the 3rd and 4th) our addition will look like this:

Ex.151

Notice that care has been taken to score the horns so that they overlap both the lower cornets and the upper trombones, tieing both sections together. While the 3rd and 4th horns are in unison, they are doubling the melody, which is sound practice, and furthermore the note "C" (root of the chord) is the best tone to double.

The alto and tenor saxophones should be superimposed on the horns, as this is the best register for these instruments and they can add strength to the horns. The baritone and bass saxophones will double the brass baritone and bass. The scoring for saxophones would then be as follows:

4. See Horns, Instrumentation.

Ex. 152

The low reeds will be completed by scoring the E-flat alto clarinet in unison with the 1st alto saxophone, and the bass clarinet and bassoon in unison on the top bass voice.

Consideration of the high reeds; piccs., fls., E-flat and B-flat clarinets, oboes, is the next step. These instruments will be assigned to the upper treble clef and will be melodic. It is possible to score them in two ways; first, harmonized like the cornets and trombones, and second, unharmonized in the octave.

The latter method is preferred in this example as the scoring for brasses and low reeds is very full. An octave assignment of the melody for these instruments would add clarity and brilliance to the passage. In the following example (Ex. 153) this reed assignment is added to the already completed scoring.

Ex. 153

Picc., *8va* Fls., Eb Cls., I Bb Cls.

Obs. II & III, Bb Cls.
Cors.

Hns.,
Saxs.

Trbs.

Bar.
Bass

Addition of the percussion will complete our score. As this is a Spanish-South American type of number tambourines and castanets would lend color. They and the snare drum would play the rhythm as outlined by the entire band. If the bass drum and tympani did the same their resonant qualities would spoil the rhythmic crispness of the passage. They will be used to best advantage if they play only a part of the rhythmic pattern as indicated below.

Ex. 155 is presented to facilitate a closer examination of each individual instrument and the part it plays in this complete score. This is a section of the full score of El Relicario, as published, illustrating that the procedure we have followed was precisely the method used in scoring this work:

This is tutti scoring in a concerted style. All the instruments of the band are playing simultaneously, and in the same rhythm. Every band composition has passages of this type and the assignment of instruments as described, is the method used. In addition to utilizing the full compass of the band, from bass to piccolo, each family of instruments, reed and brass, is melodically and harmonically complete in itself and could exist independently. Furthermore, member groups of families, cornets, horns, saxophones, and trombones, are complete in themselves. We shall later learn that this is not essential for all band writing, but for the present it is important in that it shows the proper placement of each instrument in the scheme of the band. **WP 15-16**

It will also be noticed that almost all unison duplications have been replaced with octave duplications resulting in a greater spread of instruments. All instruments are in their best playing register and the overall balance is sound.

A few additional extracts from the scores of published works will further show the common usage of this method. (Ex. 156 and Ex. 157.)

Ex. 155

Bar.
Bs.
Solo & 1st
B♭ Cors.
2nd & 3rd
B♭ Tpts.
Flgbns.
1st & 2nd
F Hns.
3rd & 4th
Bars.
1st & 2nd
Trbs.
3rd
Bss.
Timp.
S. D.
Drs.
B. D.
Cast.
Tamb.

Ex. 156

99

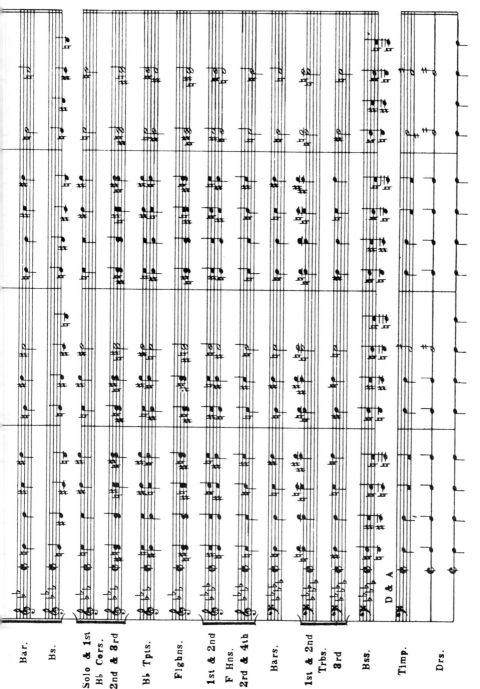

*Here the bass is not concerted but plays a rhythmic figure.

Bar.

Bss.

Solo & 1st Bb Cors.

2nd & 3rd

Bb Tpts.

Flghns.

1st & 2nd F Hns.

2rd & 4th

Bars.

1st & 2nd Trbs.

3rd

Bss.

Tlmp.

Drs.

Ex. 157

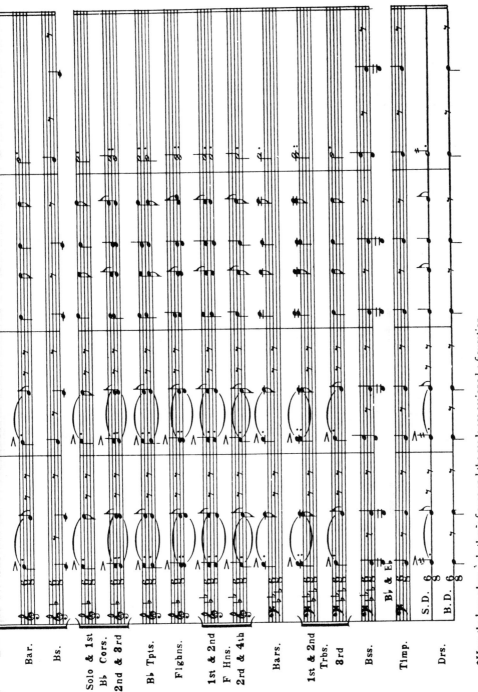

*Here the bass plays a rhythmic figure and the reeds are assigned a figuration.

SUMMATION - PART 2

To this point progression has been extremely rapid. In the space of two short chapters, beginning with the fundamentals of instrumentation, we have scored passages for full band.

Here a short period of summation is in order to assimilate the material presented. A great deal has been accomplished, and yet, very little of the technique of scoring has been covered. However, if the reader has absorbed the material presented and executed sufficient exercises, he has scored for full band.

This rapid approach to the handling of all the instruments of the full band is the initial purpose of this book. Nothing is accomplished unless it is attempted. Fear of scoring for full band, or orchestra, like composing in the larger forms, is natural. Too much time spent in writing for small ensembles is needless procrastination, and only serves to emphasize this fear. A quick cold plunge, and the ensuing shock, is necessary to gain an early ability in the handling of all instruments. Reassured of this fundamental technique, this study can be continued with greater confidence and pleasure.

In the technical presentation of this study the foregoing material constitutes the basic tools for scoring for band. The instrumental composition of the band is known, as well as the pertinent facts and character of each instrument as an individual. These instruments were first grouped into families according to timbre. This division, proving unsatisfactory for our purpose, was discarded. A division into separate voice groups, according to register, was charted. This pertinent classification offered the temporary expedient of quartet scoring for all the instruments of the full band. Execution of examples using this method illustrated the need for the creation of more than four voices. Additional voices were required to accommodate the many instruments of the band to preserve their identity and eliminate unison duplications.

A division of voices was presented, a procedure that permitted an insight into the fuller realization of the scope of the band. It offered better accommodations for the families of instruments and the member groups of these families. The procedure of tutti scoring in a concerted style was offered and executed, as outlined below:

Ex.158

1. Passage in quartet style. (open harmony)
2. Passage in quartet style. (closed harmony)
3. Assignment of Cornets and Basses.
4. Assignment of Trombones and Baritone.
5. Assignment of Horns and Saxophones.
6. Assignment of Alto, Bass Clarinets and Bassoons.
7. Assignment of high reeds.
8. Addition of percussion.

If this summation seems repetitious, it is due to the importance of this fundamental material. Do not proceed to Part 3 until you are certain that all the previous material is thoroughly understood and at your command. Execute as many examples of the concerted tutti style as possible. Be very familiar with the general placement of instruments and groups of instruments in the complete picture of the band. Take great care that all your exercises are prepared on full band score paper, all instruments in their assigned place, with proper key signatures and clefs. **WP 17**

If you have had the good fortune to hear your exercises played you are at first exhilarated, and then later, somewhat disappointed. This is good. An axiom of music is that you must be extremely self critical of your ability to achieve further success.

Your exercises undoubtedly appear monotonous both in tonal color and dynamics. Scoring for the full band in the concerted style nullifies all the individual instrumental timbre. Very little dynamic control is possible, particularly with individual instruments and groups of instruments, due to the large mass of instruments sounding.

The art of scoring is the use of instrumental tone colors and dynamics. If you have heard your examples, and feel this need, the initial purpose of this book has been achieved and we can proceed.

Part Three
DEVICES, TECHNIQUES,
AND MECHANICS OF SCORING

ACCOMPANIMENTS

Parts 1 and 2 of this book were designed so that some facility in scoring for full band could be achieved as rapidly as possible. In so doing it was necessary to bypass many of the techniques and considerations of instrumental scoring. Now that a speaking acquaintance with the instruments of the full band has been attained, we will continue by studying the individual groups of instruments in greater detail. It is necessary that much more be known of these smaller components. Careful attention to their various functions, individual and combined tone colors, and relative volume of tone, will equip us to more intelligently write for these groups.

To explore the possibilities of these small groups it is necessary that we proceed in direct opposition to the tutti concerted type of scoring already advanced. We are no longer interested in the full band and its combined tonal quality, but are seeking to discover, and cater to, the tone qualities, characteristics, and functions of each individual instrument.

SIMPLE ACCOMPANIMENTS

The simplest type of musical composition is a harmonized melody, which consists of a melodic phrase accompanied by a bass and one or more inner voices. The bass and inner voices may, or may not, be of a rhythmic character. The average popular piano sheet music has the very features we desire and will suffice for our purpose. Ex. 159 illustrates these features; a simple melody, a bass on the accented beat of the measure and rhythmic inner voices on the unaccented beats.

Ex.159

In these few measures three independent musical ideas can be recognized, two of which are subordinate to the melody. The melody is accompanied by the lower ideas in that they provide the bass and complete the harmonic structure. They further assist and compliment the melody by their contrasting rhythms.

Scoring this passage for band offers an opportunity to experiment in the use of individual instruments, and groups of instruments, whose functions and tone colors are best fitted for the assignment.

Before experimenting with instrumentation it is necessary to alter the original piano passage. As piano music the accompaniment figure in the lower part of the treble staff was written close to the melody to keep both ideas within the reach of the fingers of the right hand. This consideration has resulted in the faulty voice leading of the accompaniment figure as well as an inconsistent number of voices. (Starts with a chord of two voices and then continues with three.) It is necessary that alterations be made before assigning instrumentation.

Ex.160

In Ex. 160 the middle idea has been improved for instrumentation by rewriting for a consistent three voices with specific care as to their voicing. In its present state the passage is not playable by a pianist, but that is no concern of the orchestrator. The band has many instruments where the pianist has only ten fingers. **WP 18**

In this form the passage has obvious scoring possibilities. Let us classify the three individual ideas as Ⓐ - Ⓑ - Ⓒ , (Ex. 161) and experiment with instrumental assignments, first for brass instruments.

Ex.161

Ⓐ   Soprano register ....cornets, trumpets.
Ⓑ   Alto and Tenor register................................French horns, trombones.
Ⓒ   Bass register ....tubas.

Ⓐ could be assigned to a solo cornet, Ⓑ to three French horns, and Ⓒ to the tubas. Ⓑ might be assigned to three trombones, but it must be remembered that this volume of tone would be considerably heavier than that of the horns. However, it is safe to say that any of the possible combinations would be good scoring technique and would sound well. **WP 19**

For the reeds the possible combinations are more numerous.

Ex.162

Ⓐ   Oboes, B-flat clarinets, alto saxophones. (Piccs., flutes, and E-flat clarinets are ineffective in this range.)
Ⓑ   B-flat clarinets, alto clarinets, alto and tenor saxophones.
Ⓒ   Baritone and bass saxophones, bass clarinets and bassoons.

While the brass possibilities were limited due to the sole ability of the cornets and trumpets to play the melody, the variety of reeds available for

Ⓐ, Ⓑ, and Ⓒ offer almost limitless combinations. One hard and fast rule must be inserted here to facilitate a selection of proper balance and distinction. Regardless of the instrument (or instruments) assigned to the melody (Ⓐ), the accompaniment (Ⓑ Ⓒ) should be of contrasting tone color.

This rule can be better understood by further consideration of the construction of our passage. Ⓑ and Ⓒ constitute an accompaniment and are subordinate to the melody (Ⓐ). They support the melody by providing a bass and filling out the harmonic structure. In addition, they further enhance the rhythmic structure of the melody by a counter-rhythm of their own. The tone color of the melody will assume more distinction and individuality by assigning instruments of a contrasting tone color to Ⓑ and Ⓒ

For example, if Ⓐ were scored for clarinets, Ⓑ for clarinets and Ⓒ for bass clarinets, the assignments would be correct as to register and functions. However, the overall tone color of the passage would be monotonous. The melody would be enveloped by the similar tone color of the accompaniment and would suffer from the lack of a distinctive tone color to attain its due prominence.

We are now confronted by the choice of timbre. After we have ascertained the instruments available by virtue of register and function, we withhold the assignments until the timbre of these contenders is selected. The selection of instruments for scoring is the consideration of these three factors, and in this order: register, function and timbre.

A few possible combinations of reeds with due consideration to register, function, and timbre, are charted below. **WP 20**

Ex.163

Ⓐ	oboe	clarinets	alto sax.	oboe
Ⓑ	clarinets	sax's.	clarinets	sax's.
Ⓒ	bar. sax.	bassoons	bass cls.	bassoons

The piccolos, flutes, and E-flat clarinets have not been considered due to their ineffectiveness in the low register of the melody as written. If we refer to our technique in quartet writing it will be remembered that there is nothing to prevent us from doubling one or more of these instruments on the melody in the octave above. **WP 21**

Ex.164

(8va)	flute	oboe	clarinet	flute
Ⓐ	oboe	clarinets	alto sax.	oboe
Ⓑ	clarinets	sax's.	clarinets	sax's.
Ⓒ	bar. sax.	bassoons	bass cls.	bassoons

We have treated the two families of instruments, brass and reed, separately, and have gained an insight into the many possible combinations of tone color. These possibilities are greatly multiplied by combinations utilizing members of both families. The resultant combinations are so numerous that they cannot be listed here, but a few can be suggested.

Ex. 165

(8va)	E-flat clar.	flute	oboe	clarinets
Ⓐ	clarinets	oboe	cornet	cornets
Ⓑ	horns	horns	clarinets	trombones
Ⓒ	tubas	bsn., B cl.	bar. sax.	tubas

The combination of instruments of both families presents another consideration of assignment, balance of tone. It is obvious that combinations of all brass and all reed will be relatively well balanced in volume. Combinations consisting of both brass and reed have to be selected with greater care to preserve the balance of tone between the melody, accompanimnt, and bass. (Ⓐ - Ⓑ - Ⓒ).

In Ex. 165 the first suggested grouping of clarinets, (indicating clarinets 1, 2, and 3, — a minimum of 6 players) will balance well with the accompaniment of horns and basses. If Ⓐ were written instead for a solo clarinet, it would then be greatly overshadowed by the accompaniment. Similarly, if in the third grouping Ⓐ was scored for cornets (indicating cornets 1, 2, and 3, — a minimum of 4 players) the clarinets and bar. sax. on Ⓑ and Ⓒ would render very feeble support due to their relatively weak body of tone.

Actual choice of instrumentation is a result of the dictates of the composition being scored and the musical preference, and experience, of the orchestrator.

In general, it is safe to say the melodic timbre and overall dynamic level désired will dictate the instrumentation of the accompaniment. If a double-reed quality is desired for the melody and the dynamic level of the passage is low, perhaps mf, the accompaniment will be assigned to instruments of a contrasting tone color and subordinate dynamics. If the opposite is desired with cornets 1, 2, and 3 on the melody, the accompaniment will need be assigned to the heavier brasses like trombones and tubas, to adequately support the passage.

If instrumentation is selected with careful consideration of register, function, tone quality, and balance of tone, the passage will be well scored. However, after hearing his attempts the orchestrator may be dissatisfied with one or more of the component tone qualities. As said previously, this selection is one of the musical preference, and the sure technique of timbre selection is a result of experience.

The procedure of scoring simple accompaniments is outlined below:

Ex.166 (1) Passage to be scored.

(2) Possible alterations in passage.

(3) Assignment of melody.

(4) Assignment of accompaniment.

    (a) Contrasting tone color.

    (b) Balance of tone.

The above outline is the scoring procedure suggested for all types of melodies with simple rhythmic accompaniments. Using this outline as a guide, as many exercises as possible should be executed. All simple popular songs, marches, and waltzes are excellent subjects for this technique. Carefully scored and critically heard, these exercises will do much to develop selection of tone color and balance of tone. **WP 22**

MELODY IN TENOR REGISTER

It might be desired that the melody be assigned to some instrument not in the soprano register. In its present key, but an octave lower, the melody is in an excellent tenor register, and lies equally well for the bass instruments if written two octaves lower. To prepare this change of register for the melody it is only necessary to incorporate this idea in the second step of our outline for scoring simple accompaniments.

The original passage is again as follows:

Ex.167

The second step in our outline is the alteration of the passage for instrumentation. As we desire the melody in the tenor register, first make this change, and then add the accompaniment.

Ex.168

In the above example the melody has been written down an octave to the tenor register and the bass added exactly as in the original passage. The alto-tenor accompaniment figure, if left in its original position, would be then in the same register as the melody. These two ideas in the same register would compete with each other and the melody would be the loser in loss of distinction and lack of freedom of movement. By moving the accompaniment up an octave, both ideas retain their distinction and the melody is unimpeded in its movement. From here on the passage is scored by continuing with the third step of the outline. (Ex. 166) **WP 23**

MELODY IN BASS REGISTER

Assigning the melody to the bass register is accomplished in the same manner. First, write the melody two octaves lower to the bass register, and then add the accompaniment.

Here the melody in the bass supplants the original bass part necessitating changes in the harmonic structure of the accompaniment (bars 3 and 4). The accompaniment may remain in the original alto-tenor register or be written an octave higher in the soprano register. In either position it does not interfere with the melodic movement. The accompaniment may be written in both the alto-tenor and soprano register (as indicated) if a heavily scored passage is desired. **WP 24**

MELODY IN THE ALTO REGISTER

In its present key the melody does not lie well for an instrument in the alto register. The key of "F" (Dm) would be a good choice and we can begin scoring by writing the melody in that key for the alto register and adding the bass as in the original passage. Again, as with the tenor register example the accompaniment figure is in the same register as the melody and must be written above or below. In Ex. 170 the accompaniment is written above the melody. **WP 25**

DEVELOPMENT OF ACCOMPANIMENTS

The basic art of the orchestrator is the scoring of a given piece of material for instrumental ensemble. The assignment of instruments with careful regard to color and relative volume of tone is the subject of this study. However, this study would be incomplete if we were not to discuss, however briefly, the creativeness of orchestration.

Every composition, large or small, simple or elaborate, is comprised of three elements; melody, harmony, and rhythm. The melody is the theme, the focal point of the composition. It is the dominating element and will permit no tampering or alteration. The elements of harmony and rhythm are subordinate to the melody and may be modified by the orchestrator for the purpose of providing a better setting for the melody.

The good orchestrator is the one that uses his skill to the fullest extent in assigning instrumentation. The great orchestrator goes beyond this and also exercises his inventiveness with the material at hand. Casual listening to the instrumental ensembles of the Radio, Screen, and Records will illustrate this point. They all compete on an even basis in offering the contemporary songs. The success of each ensemble lies in the individuality of presentation. If the material is a common factor with all, how can any distinction be attained?

Their stock in trade, individuality, lies in the manner of presentation. This essence of individuality that leads you to prefer one ensemble to another is the style of presentation; excellence and quality of performance, instrumental and vocal soloists, orchestrations.

In these orchestrations the writers are not only concerned with the instrumentation of a passage. They also alter the material in accordance with their ideas of presentation. The original accompaniment material may be altered harmonically or rhythmically.

RHYTHMIC ELABORATION

In example 171 our original accompaniment example (Ex. 160) is restated again using the symbols Ⓐ , Ⓑ and Ⓒ to indicate the three separate ideas. Their rhythms are graphically illustrated. **WP 26**

A little experimentation and inventiveness with the rhythms of the accompaniment, Ⓑ and Ⓒ , will produce interesting results.

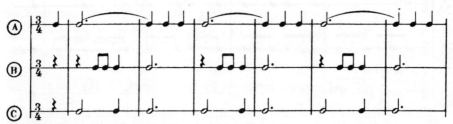

These are but a few of the rhythmic alterations possible even with this rather obvious passage. Notice particularly that the odd bars (1-3-5) receive the greatest rhythmic treatment while the even bars are relatively static. Also notice that the melody has its greatest movement (rhythmically) on the even bars and is sustained on the odd bars. Too much rhythmic movement in the accompaniment while the melody moves, impedes and competes with its free flow. Simultaneous rhythmic activity of the melody and accompaniment destroys the distinctiveness of both. When the melody is at rest the accompaniment may aspire to rhythmic interest and vice versa. This is a fundamental rule of all accompaniments and should be strictly observed. **WP 27**

An example in 6/8 meter.

Ex. 173

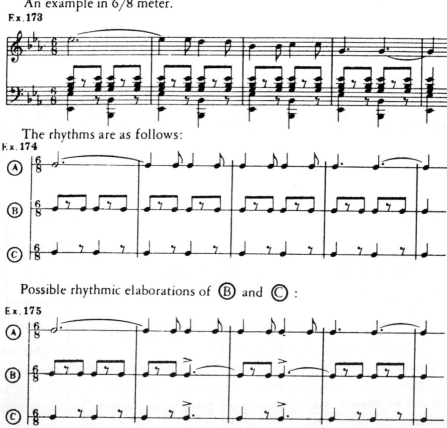

The rhythms are as follows:

Ex. 174

Possible rhythmic elaborations of (B) and (C) :

Ex. 175

All accompaniments, regardless of meter, can be rhythmically elaborated. Inventiveness in this phase of writing is permitted the orchestrator and will greatly assist in the overall interest and quality of his work. Paper and pencil are the only materials needed for these exercises as we are concerned only with rhythms. Select any melody from memory and record its rhythm. Add a simple bass and accompaniment, Ⓑ Ⓒ , and with this as a basic plan see how many rhythmic variations you can invent. **WP 28**

The basic rhythms of "Yankee Doodle" are as follows:

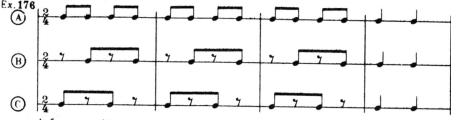

A few possible rhythmic variations.

HARMONIC ELABORATION

In working with the harmonic elements of a composition the orchestrator does not have the same freedom that was permitted with the rhythmic elements. The basic harmonic structure of a composition is as vital as the melody and may not be altered. Many orchestrators precede their scoring by calmly reharmonizing the composition. This is the sphere of the composer, and not the orchestrator. Good or bad, the harmonic structure is the setting for the melody and both are interdependent. Devoid of its original harmonic structure, and forced to depend upon another for support, a melody immediately loses its character. A few experimental reharmonizations of well known popular songs, folk tunes, and hymns, will clearly illustrate this point.

Although the basic structure is not to be altered, certain modifications are permitted. The devices of composition; passing tones, added tones, suspensions, and anticipations, are available to the orchestrator. We can begin by employing our newly developed rhythmic technique on the harmonic structure. The original example is again stated: **WP 29**

Ex.178

The accompaniment components, Ⓑ Ⓒ , might be combined to spell out the harmonic content in an arpeggio fashion.

Ex.179

The basic harmonic structure has not been altered, but its components have been modified to provide a more flowing accompaniment with less rhythmic impact. The following might be used if slightly more rhythm were desired.

Ex.180

Here neighboring tones have been utilized to soften the original strong rhythmic pattern. This procedure might be further elaborated to include all the voices of the accompaniment.

Ex.181

or

Many famous melodies in their original piano form are quite uninteresting from an instrumental view. The accompaniment seems much too stiff for the following melody.

Ex.182

An arpeggio treatment of the accompaniment renders it much more compatible to the style of the melody.

Ex.183

Another slightly more rhythmic treatment is as follows:

Ex.184

Here again, an upper neighboring tone has been utilized to soften the rhythmic impact as well as provide more rhythmic and harmonic variety.

Note in these examples that the accompaniment, however altered, never competes rhythmically with the melody. All of the harmonic elaborations take place when the melody is at rest. It is the desire of the orchestrator to enhance the melody by providing it with an interesting setting and not to interfere with its activity. **WP 30**

COUNTERMELODIES

Countermelody is another device of the composer that is of great help to the orchestrator. It is as the name implies, a melody written against (as in counterpoint) the line and rhythm of the main melody. It should not impede or compete with the main melody as its function is one of support and additional interest. It is classified as an accompaniment device; a more highly developed form of the inner voice idea typified as Ⓑ in the preceding section on accompaniments.

Early band music is characterized by an overemphasis and misuse of countermelodies. The baritones, for example, were regarded as existing in the band solely for the purpose of playing melodies, arpeggios, and figurations totally apart from the balance of the band. This tradition is still adhered to today in the final section of marches, where the baritones, occasionally supported by trombones and low woodwind, play countermelodies of very pronounced independence.

Properly and intelligently used, countermelodies are a great aid to the orchestrator, but great care and taste should be exercised in their construction and presentation to avoid exaggeration of their importance. Every device of orchestration, including instrumental timbre, should be used with discretion and clarity of purpose. Careless and flagrant use soon tends to minimize the effectiveness of these devices, lessening their value to the orchestrator.

Countermelodies are an accompaniment device and are governed by the same general rules. They should contrast with the main melody in both register and timbre. Furthermore, their rhythmic activity is restricted by the movement of the melody to which they are counter. For greatest effectiveness and support the countermelody should move when the melody rests and vice versa.

It may be observed that the sum total of all these general rules is to insure the subordination of the countermelody to the main melody. At no time should it assume characteristics of such importance that it becomes more interesting than the theme of the composition. All its components of rhythm, melody, timbre, and dynamics should be subordinate to the theme as its main function is one of support and added interest. **WP 31**

The simplest countermelody is a single tone, similar to an organ point. The usual function of a sustained tone of this type is one of cohesion. It serves as a "string" to tie together the other elements of the passage.

Ex.185

A further example of this sustained type is the simple diatonic scale exhibited below. Its long, leisurely, legato line has a binding effect on the rapid movement of the theme and the rhythmic support of the accompaniment.

A countermelody with a more pronounced melodic contour is presented in Ex. 187. The main melody is scored for cornets and trombone, played staccato, and the countermelody is a legato oboe solo. While the similarity of registers is a violation of one of the general rules, the countermelody still contrasts strongly with the theme in its rhythmic, melodic and dynamic construction.

Later in the same arrangement this countermelody is again stated, this time by the horn.

Occasionally inner harmonic voices will develop melodic characteristics that can be developed into effective countermelodies. The one illustrated below is a harmonic voice of such melodic content that it is a pleasing and effective entity in itself and renders great service in enhancing the melody.

Countermelodies may assume a canonic character and be a direct imitation of the main melody. In the following example the countermelody answers the theme a quarter-note later. While this is an unusual application of the device all the requirements are met as there is contrast in register, timbre, and activity.

The leading line of a harmonic accompaniment may be developed melodically for greater interest. In the following statement there is a pleasing melodic line to the cornet and trombone accompaniment.

In Ex. 192 the harmonic and rhythmic components are exactly the same, but the accompaniment does not have as much interest as the melodic leading of the top voice is missing.

Ex.192

The example below illustrates the same ensemble of cornets and trombones, this time legato, answering the melody in a graceful flowing fashion.

Ex.193

Contained in the harmonic structure of every musical composition are many available countermelodies. Regardless of their complexity they should all be carefully constructed as a complete melodic idea, and in addition, be a good contrapuntal voice to the theme.

There are no set rules for the creation and employment of countermelodies. Careful analysis of the construction and style of the accompaniment, as well as the melody will indicate the necessity of this device. Contrast in timbre, activity and rhythm are the guiding factors. If the melody is legato a staccato countermelody is indicated; if the melody is staccato, a long flowing countermelody will provide the greatest support and interest. **WP 32**

FIGURATIONS

Figurations are another accompaniment device closely related to countermelodies. Their duration is considerably shorter than countermelodies, sometimes only two or three notes, and they are frequently more valued for their rhythmic, rather than melodic, content. As another accompaniment device they are governed by the same general rules. Contrast in timbre, register, and activity is essential. Like countermelodies they may exist in a single solo line, or be harmonized in two, three, or even more parts, for a complete section of the band.

Figurations are perhaps the most frequently used of all scoring devices. The orchestrator feels a constant need for short fragmentary passages, both rhythmic and melodic, to heighten a melodic line, intensify a rhythmic pattern, or contrast a tonal color. This device has endless uses and is an invaluable aid for helping interest and brilliance. **WP 33**

In the example below the figuration for piccolo and flute in the fourth and fifth bars is utilized to sustain interest while the melody rests. It is equally valued for its rhythmic as well as melodic qualities.

Ex.194

The following extract illustrates the use of a harmonized figuration that has many functions. It provides movement while the melody rests, establishes the harmonic structure, and adds rhythmic interest. This passage would be complete without the figuration, but the assistance and color it contributes is obvious.

Ex.195

Rapid figurations of strongly marked melodic and rhythmic content have great intensity and are a vital driving force to a passage. The figuration in Ex. 196 is a strong element of excitement in the passage both melodically and rhythmically. Notice that the quarter note rest in the beginning of the bar permits the figuration an entrance of greater impact. Further, this entrance does not impede the melodic flow as it is initiated when the melody rests.

Ex.196

Similar examples:

Ex.197

Ex.198

Figurations of a purely rhythmic character, with little or no melodic movement, are frequently employed for added interest to a legato and flowing passage. In the passage below the trumpet*[1] figurations add a strong rhythmic drive to the sustained clarinet countermelody.

Ex.199

The brass chords in Ex. 200 emphasize the crisp, harmonic qualities of boogie-woogie music. Their activity is in sharp contrast to the balance of the passage.

Ex.200

1. Note that trumpets are used, rather than cornets, for the brilliant quality of tone desired.

Rapid reiteration of short rhythmic patterns scored for unison, octave, or harmonized groups, has a very decisive rhythmic drive.

Figurations are often combined with countermelodies for added interest. In the example below all accompaniment devices are utilized. Melody in flutes, E-flat clarinets, and xylophone; figuration in clarinet and oboe; countermelody in cornet 2 and trombone 3; and simple rhythm in horns and basses.

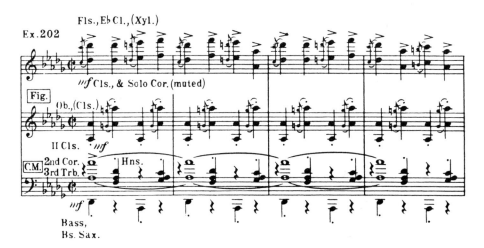

The percussion are often used for figurations of a purely rhythmic character. The xylophone, illustrated below, greatly enhances the passage with its percussive rhythmic quality.

Ex.203

The following percussion figurations are invaluable for their distinctive timbre as well as their dry rhythmic qualities.

Ex.204

Ex.205

Ex. 206

Ex. 206

The percussion instruments are occasionally added to other sections of the band to emphasize or sharpen a rhythmic figuration. **WP 34**

Ex. 207

Ex. 208

CUEING AND CROSS CUEING

Most scoring for band is of a special nature. It is done for a definite assignment and scored for a particular band. Occasionally, however, these arrangements or transcriptions are loaned to other bands (of unknown instrumentation) or submitted to publishers for print. Under these circumstances the special nature of the material may be a handicap as the instrumentation of the band for which it was originally written may be inferior or superior to that of other bands, or not considered as "average" by publishers.

All scoring for band should be done for the complete band instrumentation even though the particular band for which the work is being scored does not meet this standard. If an arranger scores only for the instruments at hand he is missing the opportunity of fully learning the use of all instruments and when those he does not use become available, he will be unsure of his technique. It should be remembered that it is always easier to eliminate (tacet) an instrument than it is to add one.

In view of the foregoing it is necessary that all band scoring be executed in a practical manner so that it can be adequately performed by all bands, regardless of instrumentation. The basic instruments of the band; flutes, clarinets, cornets, trumpets, trombones, baritones, sax's, basses, and drums are common to all ensembles even though their numbers and proportions may vary. The other instruments completing the instrumentation of the band; E-flat clarinets, oboes, bassoons, alto and bass clarinets, bass clarinets, "F" horns, contra bassoons, and contra bass clarinets are unknown quantities. Some bands boast all of these instruments, others a few, and to insure performance by the greatest majority any important passages scored for these instruments must be indicated elsewhere in the ensemble. The notation of the part of one instrument, on the part of another, is called "cueing."

Throughout the condensed score examples in this text the reader will notice instrumentation indicated in brackets (). A notation viz: Bsn. (Bs. Cl.) is a visual indication that the passage is scored for bassoon, but in the event that a bassoon is not present the passage is also written in the bass clarinet part where it is available for performance. The bassoon is "cued" in the bass clarinet part and the bass clarinet has a bassoon "cue."

In the following passage there are three sets of cues. The desired instrumentation consists of oboe, clarinets 2 and 3, bassoons, and bass clarinets. However, by using cues the arrangement could be played by bands not having either oboes, bassoons, or bass clarinets.

On the full score, and the parts, these cues are notated as follows:

Note that the cues are identified with the names of the originating instruments and written in small notes. The obvious difference between the large notes of the performers regular part and these small notes, is a clear indication that the cued passage is only to be played in the absence of the instrument for which it is scored. To further indicate that the small notes are cues each bar is marked with a full bar rest.

Cross (or secondary) cueing is the method of notating a second substitute instrument if there is any doubt of the availability of the first. The following example illustrates a bassoon solo cued in the tenor sax and baritone horn.

Ex.211

The tenor sax and baritone are not simultaneous, but progressive cues. In the absence of the bassoon the tenor sax plays the passage. However, if there is no tenor sax the baritone horn also has the passage. The score and parts are indicated as follows:

Ex.212

The cue in the tenor sax is simply marked with the originating instrument. However, the second substitute instrument, baritone, is marked (Bsn. Ten. Sax) indicating that the cue is to be played only in the absence of both the bassoon and tenor sax. **WP 35**

All published band works are scored for a mythical "average" band. While the instrumental composition of this ensemble varies slightly with arrangers and composers of its material, the general conception is as follows. The instruments in the left column are basic and included in all bands. Those in the right column enable the band to achieve symphonic proportions, but are not always present.

Ex. 213

BASIC INSTRUMENTS	SYMPHONIC INSTRUMENTS
Piccolos	Oboes
Flutes	English Horns
B-flat Clarinets	Alto Clarinets
Bass Clarinets	Contra Bass Clarinets
Alto Sax.	Bassoons
Tenor Sax.	Contra Bassoons
Baritone Sax.	Bass Sax.
Cornets	Fleugelhorns
Trumpets	
Horns (F and E-flat) [2]	
Baritones	
Trombones	
Basses (E-flat and B-flat)	
Drums	

For practical writing and to insure performance by the majority of bands all important passages for symphonic instruments must be cued in one or more of the basic instruments. The choice of a cueing instrument depends upon the register of the original passage, as well as its quality and quantity of tone. A solo for bassoon in its middle register could be cued for tenor sax., baritone sax., bass clarinet, trombone, or baritone. However, if it is a light and graceful passage accompanied by horns, the trombone and baritone would be unsuitable as cueing instruments because of their quality and quantity of tone. Similarly the baritone sax. is unsatisfactory and the actual choice rests between the bass clarinet and tenor sax. with the former preferred.

The chart below suggests some of the instruments available, due to corresponding compass, for cueing the symphonic instruments. It is not intended, or to be used, as a reference chart. The arranger should cue and cross cue his work according to its structure and circumstances will occasionally force him to create substitutions other than these suggested.

Ex. 214

	Flute
Oboe_____	B-flat Clarinet
	Muted Trumpet
	Bassoon
	Oboe
English Horn_____	Bassoon
	Alto Saxophone
	Horn (F or E-flat)

2. A recent survey by the author indicates that the instrumentation of the average band includes a minimum of three horns. However this number is usually a combination of both "F" and "E-flat" instruments.

E-flat Clarinet_____	Piccolo
	Flute
	B-flat Clarinet

Alto Clarinet_____	B-flat Clarinet
	Bass Clarinet
	Alto or Tenor Sax.
	Horn (F or E-flat)

Contra Bass Clarinet_____	Bass Clarinet
	Bass Sax.
	Contra Bassoon
	Bass

Bassoon_____	Bass Clarinet
	Tenor or Baritone Sax.
	Baritone
	Trombone
	Bass

Contra Bassoon_____	Bassoon
	Bass Sax.
	Contra Bass Clarinet
	Bass

Bass Saxophone_____	Baritone Sax.
	Contra Bassoon
	Contra Bass Clarinet
	Bass

Fleugelhorn_____	Cornet
	Horn (F or E-flat)
	Baritone
	Trombone

All bands do not have complete percussion sections and when any of these effects are important, substitutes should be indicated and cued. **WP 36**

Ex. 215

Chimes_____	cued for _____	Bells
Tympani _____	cued for _____	Bass Drum (Rhythm only)
Xylophone _____	cued for _____	Piccolo, Flute, B-flat Clar.
Temple Blocks_____	cued for _____	Wood Blocks
Tom-Toms _____	cued for _____	Muffled Snare Drum

In addition to using this notation for availability of instruments it is also advisable to cue passages, even when scored for basic instruments, that make unusual technical demands of the instrumentalist. The solo for horns in the following example is cued for saxophone for this reason. Horns are present in all bands, but this particular passage demands ability on the instrument that may be beyond the average performer. However, the passage is quite easy for saxophones.

Ex.216

Flutes are also available in all bands, but the following solo is quite difficult for the average player. For the oboe, it is comparatively simple. **WP 37**

Ex.217

GENERAL PROCEDURE OF SCORING

Before progressing to Part 4 and the various types of band scoring it is necessary that an efficient work procedure be outlined. There is only one way to score and that is with an orderly and logical consideration of the steps involved. They are as follows:

(1) Selection of Material.
(2) Form.
(3) Key Consideration.
(4) Condensed Score.
(5) Full Score.

Regardless of the type of writing, this is the General Procedure of Scoring. Detailed presentation of these steps will illustrate that some are more important in transcription than arrangements, and vice versa. However, for an orderly and constructive working procedure, scoring, in every case, should begin with step 1 and end with step 5.

SELECTION OF MATERIAL

The care and time expended in the selection of material is an important part of scoring and makes all other steps relatively simple. A superficial examination of material for a given assignment may lead to later complications when the arranger or transcriber will be confronted with passages that actually defy scoring.

TRANSCRIPTION

Extreme care should be exercised in the selection of orchestral material for band transcription. The instrumentation of the band is not suitable for the performance of all orchestral material and only what can be adequately scored should be attempted.. Examine the score carefully for the following devices that are extremely difficult to transcribe.

(1) Independent activity of w.w. and strings in the upper register.

(2) Intricate and delicate passages for violas, cellos, and basses.

(3) Passages for strings of a "violinistic" character with rapid skips, changes of register, double stops, spiccato bowing, etc.

ARRANGING

The selection of material for arrangements is not subject to the restrictions pertinent to transcriptions. Piano, choral, and organ literature, as well as popular music, exhibits no definite instrumental color and can be scored in accordance with the taste and skill of the arranger. Except for certain pianistic devices, none of this material contains any construction difficult to score for band. As arranging is largely creative, the arranger can accept, reject, or modify any component of these compositions (as well as create new material) for the presentation of his ideas.

The selection of material for arrangements is usually based on the

(4) String phrases of unusually long duration and sustained intensity.

(5) Passages for harp and piano.

If an orchestral score contains all or many of these characteristics it is not a good subject for band transcription. However, if only a few are present and can be transcribed by compromise or substitution, the material has possibilities and should be examined further.

need for special material that is not available in print. School or folk songs, for assemblies or outdoor concerts, suggest one type of material. Medleys of popular songs from shows or motion pictures suggest another type, and a need for solo material for some gifted (perhaps technically limited) instrumentalist, still another. There exists a wealth of material for the above, or any other needs, and selection is based mainly on adaptability of material. **WP 38**

FORM

The material should now be examined for its form of composition. Analyze the work for its compositional devices of themes, counter themes, codettas, development, etc. Observe the notations and markings that are an indication of these devices. Letters or numbers that are circled or squared (A ㊲ Ⓑ 29) usually indicate basic elements for form. Double bar lines, repeated sections, first and second endings, and changes of key are further signs of structure.

Note particularly the instrumentation the composer has utilized in presenting his material and decide how much can be retained or what substitutions can be made.

Group, or re-group these components into the desired form, and to the required length, adding necessary introductions, interludes and endings. **WP 39**

KEY CONSIDERATION

The considerations of the two previous steps have indicated that a transcription is practical, as well as outlining sectionally how the work is to be scored. We are now concerned with the key of the composition.

Orchestral keys are usually selected for the convenience of its most important family of instruments, the strings. The violin is so constructed and fingered as to be at ease in sharp keys. The clarinets are

In contrast to the transcriber who assigns instruments for their ability to perform a definite passage in a set key, the arranger has considerably more freedom. As said before, the material available for arrangements rarely exhibits any preference of instrumental color. Furthermore, composed for keyboard or choral ensembles the keys were selected after due consideration of the sonorities, registers and facilities of these mediums.

usually the recipients of string passages in band transcriptions, and as they are constructed in flat keys (B-flat, E-flat), a change of key is often, but not always, necessary. Having less facility than a string instrument, the clarinet is sufficiently taxed in performing these passages without being additionally burdened with a difficult key necessitating involved fingering. The art of orchestration is in practical scoring and all possible skill should be utilized in writing each part so that it is "on the instrument" and within the ability of the performer. This consideration is particularly pertinent in transcription as the material was originally conceived for orchestra and an adequate band scoring demands that all transference be skillfully affected.

Any transposition for the benefit of clarinets will naturally affect all other instruments of the band. With a tentative transposition in mind, the score should again be analyzed noting how all other instruments are affected. If any instruments are led to the extremes of their compasses, or any passages are in difficult registers, the tentative key is unsatisfactory and another should be attempted.

For orchestral music in sharp keys the most practical band transcription is a semitone higher or lower.

Ex.219

The band arranger is in no way committed to these keys as he is working with an entirely different medium with its own peculiar characteristics. The key consideration of arranging is actually in direct opposition to that of transcription as the instruments are assigned first, and then set in a tonality (key) in which they can best perform these assignments.

As the majority of brass and woodwind instruments are built in flat keys these keys are the best selection for the most effective and practical band scoring.

Ex.218

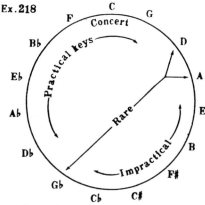

Of all band instruments the clarinet is one of the most important, occupying a position similar to that of the first violin in the orchestra. Like the violin, the clarinet is an agile instrument and intrusted with passages of technique and speed. In view of this the clarinet should be the first instrument consulted when setting a key.

Aside from the primary use of keys for the best placement of in-

This nearby transposition puts the band in flat keys and rarely affects the register or compass of any instrument.

struments, the arranger can use this change of tonality as an additional scoring device. In the hands of a skilled worker this is perhaps the most effective and colorful of all devices. As presented and exemplified in the Summation of Part 3 the reader will recognize its creative possibilities for added interest, brilliance, and abrupt change of mood.

CONDENSED SCORE
WP 40

In steps 1, 2, and 3 all the actual arranging has been done, even if only mentally. Material has been selected, formed, instruments tentatively assigned and the key (or keys) selected. The writing of the condensed score (sketch) in concert key is simply a detailed recording of this work so that it may be better evaluated in its entirety. This condensed score should be written on ordinary ten or twelve manuscript paper using two, three, (or more) bracketed staves if necessary. Two are occasionally sufficient for simple scoring, but three are the average as they allow for a clearer notation of the instrumentation and ideas. In the three staff system the instruments of the band are generally notated in the areas indicated below.

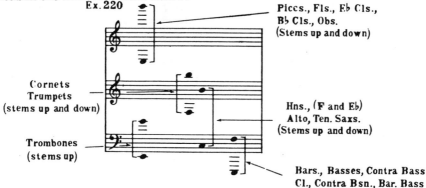

Ex. 220

Piccs., Fls., Eb Cls., Bb Cls., Obs. (Stems up and down)

Cornets Trumpets (stems up and down)

Hns., (F and Eb) Alto, Ten. Saxs. (Stems up and down)

Trombones (stems up)

Bars., Basses, Contra Bass Cl., Contra Bsn., Bar. Bass

If the arrangement is intricate with many independent scoring ideas more staves will be needed. These should be added only when necessary and then eliminated to return to a two or three staff system.[4] Any combination of clefs necessary for a clear exposition of the work is permitted.

Full scores are seldom published for band music and the band leader must use this condensed version for conducting. Similar to a piano reduction it is, at best, a weak and vague indication of the scoring. With this inadequacy in mind every care should be exercised to notate with clarity and detail the

4. See Ex. 227.

structure and instrumentation of the work. Stems must be up and down for the different instrumental groups and these should be clearly marked to show the instruments they contain. Dynamics, phrasing, and breath markings must be carefully notated and only for those instruments to which they apply. The numerous examples of condensed scores throughout this text should be sufficient to illustrate their proper construction.

FULL SCORE

Using the condensed score as a sketch the work is now transferred to the full score page. Each instrument is transposed to its own key in its own clef. The score should be neat and orderly and contain sufficient rehearsal numbers or letters to aid the conductor. Score paper without bar lines is preferred so the width of the measure can be adjusted to accommodate passages of many notes without crowding. All parts should be written with careful regard to the time value of notes and their proper placement in the measure. The following examples will show how difficult it is to read even a condensed score when the spacing and placement of notes is sloppily done. **WP 41**

Ex. 221

Ex.222

SUMMATION - PART 3

The foregoing material, however briefly presented, constitutes all of the basic techniques of scoring for band. Good scoring is the result of skillful and imaginative use of the few devices illustrated, coupled with a constant search for new uses and combinations. While the two general headings of tutti and accompaniment include all the basic techniques, it is not possible to list or even guess the scoring combinations possible when they are multiplied by the factors of tonal, harmonic, melodic, dynamic, and rhythmic contrast.

These basic devices should be clearly understood and easily manipulated. Their use should be almost intuitive, much the same as the motions of driving a car. It is even more important that these constructional elements of scoring be readily catalogued when heard and seen. In striving for speed, clarity and individuality of style, these devices must be practiced constantly to develop the same facility that a performer has with his instrument.

Cultivate the searching habit of looking beyond the melody. The instrumental assignment of the melody, while of prime importance, requires the least technique. The skilled listener and orchestrator devotes only a fraction of his attention to the melody. The structural elements of the composition that lie beyond the theme are the material on which the orchestrator exercises his skill and personality. This is the bare canvas of the painter; the wet clay of the sculptor, the ground plan of the architect. This is the material to be patterned, colored, and set in motion for the sole purpose of providing a setting for the melody.

Careful analysis of instrumental music, orchestra as well as band, will quickly develop the facility of recognizing component structural elements. A theme is presented in full or partial tutti or it is accompanied or both. Basically, there is no other approach. The art of scoring is the manner, skill, and style of this presentation.

The following pages present the complete condensed score of Yankee Doodle for the purpose of analyzing its structural composition and scoring devices. Structurally the work is a set of instrumental variations on a theme of sixteen bars. For greater contrast of material the theme has been divided into its component parts (antecedent and consequent phrases), and each is occasionally elaborated without due regard for its relation to the other. The middle section of the composition presents new, original material, in place of a development of the original theme.

For a better understanding of the material construction of this composition, devoid of instrumentation, the themes are illustrated and labeled 1, 2 and 3, and their use and alteration is analyzed in outline form.

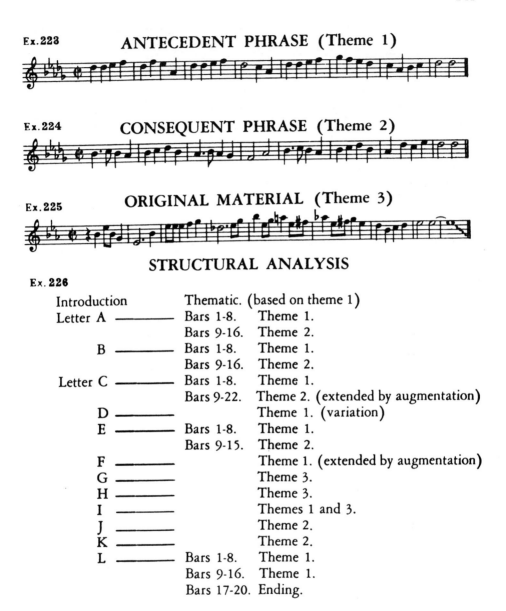

Ex.223   **ANTECEDENT PHRASE** (Theme 1)

Ex.224   **CONSEQUENT PHRASE** (Theme 2)

Ex.225   **ORIGINAL MATERIAL** (Theme 3)

STRUCTURAL ANALYSIS

Ex.226

Introduction	Thematic. (based on theme 1)	
Letter A ————	Bars 1-8.	Theme 1.
	Bars 9-16.	Theme 2.
B ————	Bars 1-8.	Theme 1.
	Bars 9-16.	Theme 2.
Letter C ————	Bars 1-8.	Theme 1.
	Bars 9-22.	Theme 2. (extended by augmentation)
D ————		Theme 1. (variation)
E ————	Bars 1-8.	Theme 1.
	Bars 9-15.	Theme 2.
F ————		Theme 1. (extended by augmentation)
G ————		Theme 3.
H ————		Theme 3.
I ————		Themes 1 and 3.
J ————		Theme 2.
K ————		Theme 2.
L ————	Bars 1-8.	Theme 1.
	Bars 9-16.	Theme 1.
	Bars 17-20.	Ending.

From the above outline it will be seen that theme 1 is stated ten times, theme 2 six times, and theme 3 twice. The entire composition is composed of the alteration and reiteration of the three themes totaling twenty-four bars.

Here is where the art of scoring comes to the fore. A simple experiment of playing these three themes on the piano in the outline order would show that the material in this state is monotonous, colorless, and devoid of sustained interest. The instrumental scoring of this material provides all these lacking qualities.

Another look at the score of this composition, this time analyzing the scoring devices used, will clearly illustrate the contributions of the orchestrator. The circled numerals in the score indicate the devices, which are analyzed in the footnotes.

This score contains all the devices presented in this book. Further, the devices themselves are varied in the manner of presentation by the use of timbre, harmonic, and rhythmic contrasts. The fundamental device of full and partial tutti is present in many forms. There are tuttis for brass, brass and horns; horns, sax's, trombones alone; trombones and horns, and woodwind alone. The accompaniment devices are treated with even more variety, some of a complicated and stylized nature and others having simply a very elemental rhythmic function.

In this score the changes of key are a very important scoring device. The changes of key are here, as always, determined by two desires; a change in pitch or key feeling; a better placement for instrumental registers (both melody and accompaniment).

The change of key at B from D-flat to C is due to a desire for a raised key feeling to brighten the new passage. It is not dictated by instrumental registers as B could just as well be scored in D-flat. Similarly the change back to D-flat at C , and E-flat at D , is the result of a desire for a different key feeling. The change at E is necessary for the proper placement of the tutti trombones. The preceding key is unsatisfactory as the trombones would then be in an impractical register, either too high or too low. The changes at F G and L are for key feeling, each new key being higher (D, E-flat, F) heightening the interest and brilliance.

Further examination of the score will show that while theme 1 is presented ten times each statement is a different instrumental presentation and no two are alike. Themes 2 and 3 are equally varied in instrumental presentation. When any two or more successive melody or accompaniment presentations are similar, other devices are superimposed to prevent exact repetition. In J and K the melody is stated exactly the same in tutti trombones and saxes. However, at K the dynamic level is raised and the cornets and horns introduce a figuration. Similarly at H the accompaniment is an exact repetition of G but the melody and figuration is varied at the latter letter.

Critical analyzation of structural construction and scoring devices is a pertinent factor in creating facility in orchestration. These elements are present in all mediums of composition; orchestra, band, organ, piano, etc. Almost all publishers include a condensed score in every band and orchestra publication and these may be purchased separately. With the foregoing analysis as a guide, as many scores as possible should be carefully analyzed.

Facile recognition and use of these structural and scoring devices will greatly assist in the initial steps of scoring for band. When the material to be scored, regardless of its complexity, can be clearly recognized in terms of its component elements, and the relative importance of these to each other established, the professional approach has been attained. **WP 42**

YANKEE DOODLE

Ex. 227

5. Tutti scoring for full band.

6. Tutti scoring for full band. The woodwinds play a simplification of the melody for a sustained legato, line.
7. Figuration presenting rhythmic contrast.
8. Melody in octaves, harmonized in thirds for contrast to the preceding tutti.
9. Tutti brass, sax's, and horns. Clarinets supplying simple accents.

10. Figuration for rhythmic contrast.
11. Simple rhythm accompaniment in horns and one trombone.
12. Variation of theme 2, tutti woodwind.
13. Tutti brass (muted) accompaniment. Note use of low w.w. for bass. The muted brass would be completely overbalanced by a brass bass.

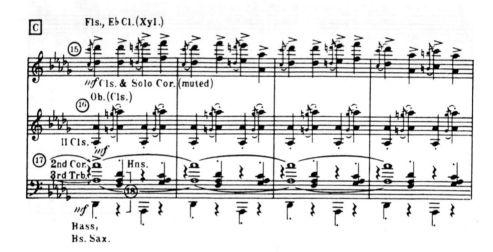

14. Solo cornet supporting clarinets an octave lower.
15. Melody in w.w., solo cornet (8 basso), and xylophone. The grace notes are for accentuation of the first and third beats.
16. Figuration.
17. Countermelody. Note that the countermelody and figuration are based on the same tones.
18. Simple rhythmic accompaniment.

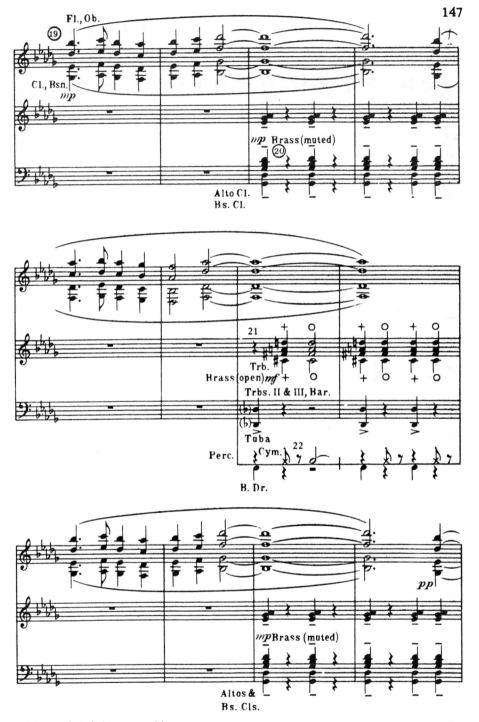

19. Solo woodwinds in open position.
20. Rhythmic accompaniment of tutti brass (muted) and low reeds.
21. Tutti brass (open) rhythmic accompaniment. The symbols (+ o) indicate respectively, hand in. bell and open.
22. Percussion support to the rhythm of the accompaniment.

23. Countermelody, diatonic line.
24. Variation of theme 1.
25. Simple rhythmic accompaniment.
26. One chord figuration for phrase accent.
27. Woodwind figuration.
28. Tutti horns and trombones.

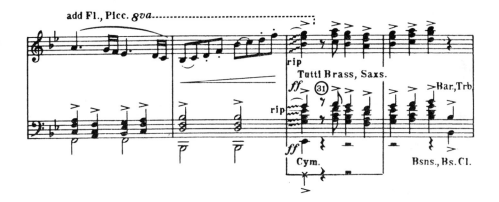

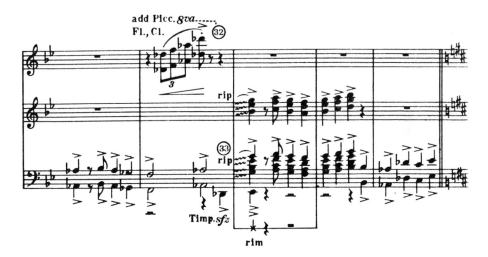

29. Figuration.
30. Countermelody. Here is a pronounced melodic line in contrast to the movement at 29 which is purely for rhythmic contrast.
31. Full band tutti.
32. Figuration, purely rhythmic.
33. Full band tutti.

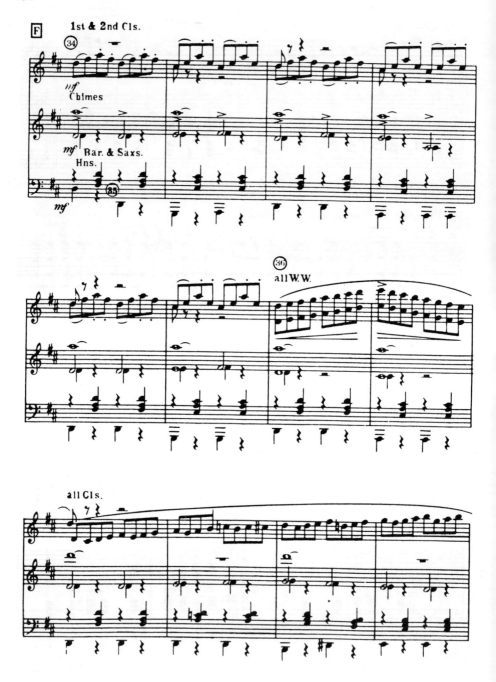

34. Figuration. Alternated between first and second clarinets to prevent fatigue.
35. Simple rhythmic accompaniment.
36. Figuration. While this line assumes the character of a countermelody its melodic quality is subordinate to its rhythmic importance.

37. Figuration.
38. Accompaniment. A two bar pattern stylized in its rhythmic, harmonic, and melodic content.
39. Melody in octaves, all cornets and trombones. An extremely powerful statement.

40. Figuration.

41. Accompaniment. Simplified version of 38.
42. Figuration.

43. Countermelody. Sustained tone.
44. Tutti trombones and sax's.
45. Countermelody. Sustained tone.
46. Figuration divided between trumpets and horns. The figure is apportioned to the trumpets who play ♫♩ ♫♩ and the horns who play ♪ ♫♩ ♫ It would be impossible for either group of instruments alone to play this eighth note figure for eight bars.

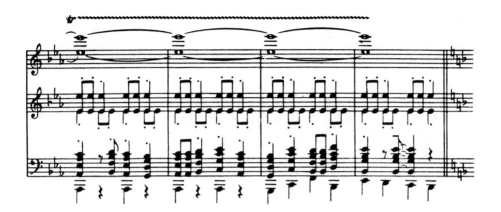

47. Figuration.
48. Tutti cornets, trombones, and sax's.
49. Simple rhythmic accompaniment.

50. Figuration. Actually a simple elaboration of the melody.
51. Tutti brass, sax's, and horns.

Part Four
TYPES OF BAND SCORING

The band repertoire is largely composed of transcriptions of orchestral material. In the early growth of the ensemble, when it began its development from a purely marching unit to its present-day symphonic proportions, suitable literature for this new ensemble was not available. Then, as now, few composers of note wrote for the band. In an attempt to secure literature that would assist in its growth to a symphonic medium, the band turned to the literature of the orchestra.

Older than the band by hundreds of years, the orchestra was, even then, slowly but surely assuming its contemporary instrumentation and its literature was plentiful and varied. This was the literature the band needed and works were selected and transcribed for the hungry new ensemble. Having little literature of its own, the new medium had a tremendous appetite. These first transcriptions were of great assistance to the growth of the band and were undoubtedly enthusiastically received. This newly-discovered font of material assisted the band in improving, enlarging and re-balancing its instrumental composition, as well as giving the new medium the much desired stature of a symphonic organization. However, the continued emphasis on transcriptions is an admission of dependence and immaturity.

A great part of orchestral literature has now been transcribed for band. When properly scored, some orchestral material is better performed by the band. Other material is adequate, and still other material is entirely unsuited for transcription and should never be (or have been) attempted.

It is hoped the foregoing views will provoke greater thought of the when and how of band transcriptions of orchestral material. The "when" is a matter of taste and beyond the province of this text. The "how" is a matter of skill and a technique of scoring for the band.

The obvious differences between the two mediums are immediately apparent. The orchestra is a string, woodwind, brass, and percussion ensemble. The band is similar, minus the string group. Furthermore, the common groups are differently composed in the two ensembles. A great staff chart of the instrumentation of the band and orchestra will illustrate other differences not quite so obvious.

The string family of the orchestra is the chief concern of the transcriber. It is complete in all registers; soprano, alto, tenor, and bass, and has great flexibility throughout the entire great staff. The extreme upper register of the strings (violins) is very important. It will be noticed in the above chart that the orchestra has two families, strings and woodwind, in this register where the band has only the single family of woodwinds. Here the strings have great strength, flexibility and distinctive timbre. It is readily understandable that orchestral passages of wind and strings, having different functions in this register, are extremely difficult to transcribe. It takes great skill and care to score in the woodwind alone of the band the difference of timbre between the strings and woodwind of the orchestra.

Furthermore, the average band does not have members in the viola and cello register to suggest the extreme flexibility and delicacy of these instruments. It is true that most bands possess alto and bass clarinets, and saxophones, (the proper instruments for this register and quality) but much experimentation is necessary to properly balance these instruments in the band ensemble. One or two alto and bass clarinets in a band are hardly sufficient to approximate the same balance in the clarinet family as exists in the string family.

The balance and strength of tone in similar registers of the two ensembles is another obvious difference. The orchestra, while not perfect, is an infinitely better balanced ensemble. The string family determines the size of the orchestra in dictating the numerical strength of the woodwind, brass, and percussion, necessary to balance the ensemble. A small body of strings needs only single wind and light brass and percussion. This is a chamber orchestra. The small symphony with more strings has double wind and slightly more brass and percussion. The full symphony with its large string section has triple or quadruple wind and full brass and percussion. The band in its present experimental stage has not, as yet, evolved a satisfactory means of self balance.

Comparison of a band and orchestra, each of approximately one hundred players, will help in analyzing the relative balance of the two ensembles.

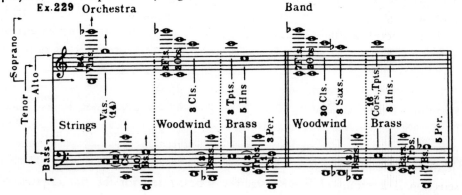

Ex. 229 Orchestra   Band

Close study of this chart will show that, register for register, the band has a greater volume of sound. If it is true that the band is capable of the greatest fortissimo this only emphasizes the fact that the orchestra is capable of the true pianissimo and therefore can boast of a superior range of dynamics.

In the soprano register the band has an equal amount of flutes, oboes and clarinets to balance the violins, flutes, oboes, and clarinets, of the orchestra. However, the 30 clarinets are much more powerful than the 24 violins. The band also has more cornets and trumpets than the orchestra plus the added family of saxophones. The band is, therefore, superior in volume of sound but is incapable of the delicacy, phrasing, and articulation of the violins in this register. Distinction of timbre between the woodwind and strings in this register is extremely difficult in band transcription, and can only be faithfully scored by careful use of flutes, oboes, and E-flat clarinets to suggest the orchestra woodwind, and B-flat clarinets to suggest violins.

In the alto register the band's numerical superiority and greater volume is even more pronounced. The violins and clarinets are barely numerically balanced and the band is infinitely greater in trombones, horns, cornets and saxophones. This register, with the tenor, is the "tubby" area of the band. This is the meeting ground for many instruments of great power, and it is in this register that the great evils of band writing are apparent, not only in transcriptions, but in all types of scoring.

In the bass register the band exhibits its greatest power and least facility and delicacy. A more careful representation and balance of bassoons, contra bassoons, bass clarinets, contra bass clarinets, and baritone and bass saxophones would do wonders for the proper transcriptions of cellos and string basses. Also, the wonderful string bass and cello device of pizzicato is lacking in the band and this is an extremely difficult problem of transcription.

This evaluation of the corresponding registers of both ensembles illustrates that the band, as it is now commonly instrumentated, is not a satisfactory medium for the performance of orchestral material. However, transcriptions form a large part of the bands literature and many more works will be transcribed. Therefore the immediate necessity is to devise ways and means of utilizing the present instrumentation of the band in transcriptions of skill and good musical taste.

The procedure of transcription begins and almost ends with a clear understanding of the instruments of the band and orchestra and their related functions. This relationship is best exemplified in the chart executed below. The instruments of the orchestra are listed in the left column and the instruments of the band best fitted to assume their functions are listed alongside. The 1st selection is a group of band instruments best fitted for the transcription of orchestra material. As some of these instruments are not present in sufficient numbers the 2nd and 3rd selection will permit the utilization of the instrumentation of the average band in making transcriptions possible and reasonably well balanced.

Ex. 280

ORCHESTRA	1ST SELECTION	2ND SELECTION	3RD SELECTION
Piccolo	Piccolos	....	....
Flutes	Flutes	....	....
Clarinets	E-flat Clarinets	B-flat Clars.	....
Oboes	Oboes	B-flat Clars.	....
Bassoons	Bassoons	Ten. Bar. Sax.	Baritone
Trumpets	Cornets, Trumpets	....	....
Trombones	Trombones	....	....
Horns (F)	Horns (F and E-flat)	Sax's.	Trombones
Tuba	Tubas (E-flat and B-flat)	....	....
Violin 1	1st B-flat and E-flat Clars.	Cornets	Flutes
Violin 2	2nd B-flat Clars.	Cornets	....
Viola	3rd B-flat and Alto Clars.	Alto. Ten. Sax.	Horns
Cello	Bass Clars.	Ten. Bar. Sax's.	Baritone
Bass	Contra Bass Clar.	Bar. Bass Sax's.	Baritone
	Contra Bassoon	Tubas	
Snare Drum	Snare Drum	....	....
Bass Drum	Bass Drum	....	....
Timpani	Timpani	....	....

The header over the band columns reads: **BAND**

These are the basic mechanics of transcriptions and by a selection of band instruments from left to right a transference of literature from orchestra can be adequately scored. **WP 43**

It is obvious that the technique does not end here even though a great many transcriptions do not exhibit any further considerations. This chart is simply an outline of the relative balance between the instruments of the band and orchestra and does not touch upon the transference of timbre, dynamics, and emotional content. However, these mechanics are basic; the initial considerations of transcription, and require more detailed discussion.

The 1st Selection constitutes an ideal band instrumentation for the execution of orchestral transcriptions. It is not an ideal band, but for the performance of orchestral material it is a collection of instruments best equipped by virtue of dynamic, timbre, and flexibility content.

The clarinet family, here complete from E-flat to contra bass, contains the maximum delicacy, shading, articulation, and unanimity of tone possible in band instruments. This family, and this family alone, is best fitted to accept the assignment of orchestral string passages. It compares favorably with the strings in delicacy and facility throughout its entire compass. The flexibility of dynamic control is good and there is a great emotional content.

Not all string writing can be transcribed for clarinets. The upper register of the violin, with its extreme flexibility, speed, and delicate dynamic shading, is beyond the possibilities of the clarinet. The violin, not having to breathe, is capable of extended phrases of great intensity which have to be interrupted, however briefly, when played on a clarinet. The spiccato of the strings, especially when continued for any length of time, or at rapid speed, is a device nontranscribable for clarinets. Rapid tonguing of a reed instrument is limited to short passages as the tongue fatigues very quickly. Sudden changes of register, easy for strings, is a facility denied the clarinetist and the colorful device of pizzicato is the sole property of stringed instruments.

Transcription of the above devices taxes the ingenuity of the transcriber in the use of substitution, compromise, and creation. The string family is the first and greatest consideration of the transcriber. Once the string parts have been assigned to band instrumentation, the balance of the transcription is easy. The band is replete in high winds and brasses and very few difficulties will be experienced in assigning these voices. If the string family is assigned first, and skillfully handled, all brass and woodwind assignments will suggest themselves easily and logically.

Contrast in timbre and dynamics is the guiding factor in transcription and is especially important in handling the orchestra strings and woodwind. We will proceed with examples of classical scoring as their simplicity and clarity will permit a more complete understanding of these basic considerations.

Ex. 231

This initial statement of the first theme of Mozart's G Minor Symphony is an example of delicacy and timbre uniformity of presentation. Execution

1. The orchestral notation "Bassi" denotes cello and bass (bass sounding an octave lower) and the band instrumentation was so assigned.

of this passage is well within the ability of clarinets and the instrumentation indicated in blocks was selected from the 1st Selection column of Ex. 230.

However, the average band is numerically deficient in alto and bass clarinets, and seldom possesses a contra bass clarinet. To execute the transcription with the instruments available we will have to consider the 2nd Selection column of Ex. 230 and make assignments from this group.

Ex. 232

	1ST SELECTION	2ND SELECTION
Violin 1	1st Clars.	1st Clars.
Violin 2	2nd Clars.	2nd Clars.
Viola	3rd Clars.	3rd Clars., Alto Sax.
Cello	Alto Clars.	Tenor Sax.
Bass	Bass Clars.	Bsns., Baritone Sax.
		Tubas

This second selection illustrates the unfitness of the average band instrumentation for the performance of orchestral material. The original delicacy and unanimity of timbre is no longer present. The single tone color of the strings is now scored for the combined colors of clarinets, saxophones, bassoons, and brass basses. This lack of the proper instruments to skillfully and tastefully transcribe the string family is the greatest problem in the transference of material from the orchestra to the band. Until the band is re-instrumentated the 2nd Selection, or at best a combination of 1st and 2nd Selection, will have to suffice.

The necessity of contrast is obvious in the following example, Ex. 233, bars thirteen to sixteen of the same movement. The entrance of the woodwind group of flute, clarinet, and bassoon, is a definite timbre contrast with the strings. The band has flutes available, but the clarinets and bassoons have already been assigned to the string transcription. Assigning the oboe to the clarinet voice of the woodwind entrance is necessary because of the preponderance of clarinet quality in the string transcription. The tenor and baritone saxophones are the second selection for bassoons, but as they are also already assigned it may be necessary to go to the 3rd Selection to transcribe the passage.

Ex. 234

ORCHESTRA	BAND		
	1ST SELECTION	2ND SELECTION	3RD SELECTION
Flute	Flute	Flute	----------------
Clarinet	Oboe	Oboe	----------------
Bassoon	Bassoon	Ten., Bar. Sax.	Baritone Horn
1st Violin	1st Clars.	1st Clars.	----------------
2nd Violin	2nd Clars.	2nd Clars.	----------------
Viola	3rd Clars	3rd Clars.	----------------
Cello	Alto Clars.	Alto, Ten. Sax.	----------------
Bass	Bass Clars.	Bsns., Bar. Sax.	----------------
	Contra Bs. Clars.	Tubas, Contra Bsn.	

Ex.233

The combination of flute, oboe, and baritone horn for the woodwind grouping is very undesirable and a re-assignment of the bassoons, and tenor and baritone saxophones will have to be undertaken to tastefully transcribe this section and preserve its contrast of timbre. The baritone horn can be eliminated by assigning the tenor and baritone saxophones to the low string transcription and reserving the bassoon for the woodwind entrance. The probable final assignment is charted in Ex. 235.

Ex.235

ORCHESTRA	BAND
Flute	Flute
Clarinet	Oboe
Bassoon	Bassoon
1st Violin	1st Clars.
2nd Violin	2nd Clars.
Viola	3rd Clars., Alto Sax.
Cello	Bass Clars., Tenor Sax.
Bass	Baritone Sax., (Tubas)

An even more insistent desire for contrast of timbre is indicated in the following passage, Ex. 236, bars 44-47. As the clarinets are assigned to the string transcription it is necessary to alter the clarinet quality in the bassoon-clarinet entrance of the second bar. Substitution of an oboe for the clarinet will preserve this contrast.

Ex.236

Ex.237

ORCHESTRA	BAND
Clarinet	Oboe
Bassoon	Bassoon
1st Violin	1st Clars.
2nd Violin	2nd Clars.
Viola	3rd Clars., Alto Clars., (Alto Sax.)
Cello	Bass Clars., Tenor Sax.
Bass	Baritone Sax., (Tubas)

While it is always advisable, and the transcriber's responsibility, to preserve a composer's instrumental color, especially in a thematic statement, it is also necessary that the contrast of color be retained. In the above assignment a modification of one was effected to preserve the other.

A similar situation presents itself in Ex. 238, bars 72-74, where the contrast of color between the 1st violins and clarinet is of extreme importance. Here, again, a compromise of substituting an oboe for the clarinet will be an effective solution.

Ex. 239

ORCHESTRA	BAND
Clarinet	Oboe
Bassoon	Bassoon
1st Violin	1st Clars.
2nd Violin	2nd Clars.
Viola	3rd Clars., Alto Clars., (Alto Sax.)
Cello	Bass Clars., (Tenor Sax.)
Bass	Baritone Sax. (Tubas)

This lengthy exposition of contrast of timbre is vitally important as it is the basis of good transcription. The band has one family of instruments (woodwinds) capable of being assigned to the orchestra's two families of woodwinds and strings. The transcriber must constantly bear in mind that the orchestral composer used these two families for their contrast of color. Not having these two sharply defined families in his ensemble, the transcriber must approximate this contrast with the instruments at his disposal.

Ex. 238

Our exercises have been limited to the G Minor Symphony of Mozart, and for a definite purpose. The classical composers regarded the orchestra as essentially a core of strings (string quintet) supported by woodwinds, brass and percussion. In the Mozart orchestral score the brass is represented by only horns and two trumpets and the percussion by just the timpani. This emphasis on strings and woodwind clearly illustrates the principle of contrast between these families. Examination of other scores of Mozart, as well as those of Beethoven and Haydn, will further show this orchestral conception and serve as study material for transcription.

The following procedure is suggested to preserve the contrast of timbre between strings and woodwinds in orchestral transcriptions: *Strings*: In transcribing the string quintet use the clarinet family, (B-flat, E-flat, bass clarinet, contra bass clarinet (contra bsn.) but excluding the small E-flat clarinet). *Woodwinds*: In transcribing the woodwinds use flutes, E-flat clarinets, oboes, and bassoons.

This procedure will not always be valid (as will any other generalization of orchestration) but will serve as a point of initial approach. When the required instrumentation is not available and it is necessary to compromise with instruments from the 2nd and 3rd Selection, do so, but only when it is absolutely necessary. Solo woodwind passages, usually for clarinet, will alter this procedure (as in Ex. 238) and necessitate a compromise. **WP 44**

ARRANGEMENTS

The process of transferring material from one musical medium or ensemble to another is called transcription. The writer prefers that this term be used only for the scoring of orchestral material for band, and that all other types of scoring be referred to as arrangements. This distinction is necessary as the term arrangement implies a certain amount of creative writing which is definitely a part of scoring piano, choral, or organ works for band. A transcription, on the other hand, requires only the skill of transferring what has been written for the instruments of the orchestra to the instruments of the band. In arrangements the original composition may be shortened or lengthened, material may be added or eliminated, sections re-harmonized, etc., changes that are definitely of a creative nature. **WP 45**

POPULAR MUSIC

In working with popular music the arranger assembles the material to create his own form. The usual popular song (chorus) is 32 bars in length and there may, or may not, be a verse. A single chorus is hardly sufficient for an arrangement and the usual procedure is to assemble a verse, two or more choruses, interspaced with transitions and modulations, all preceded by an introduction and terminated by an ending. Regardless of how composed, the form is actually one of variation, not of the melody, but of the supporting elements of composition; harmony and rhythm.

Once this outline, or form, has been decided upon, the general scoring procedure is followed, in setting the key, or keys of the arrangement, doing the condensed score and finally the full score.

In Part 3 the devices of scoring popular music for band were discussed in detail. A review of this material, along with the summation, is a necessary preparation for the further consideration of arrangements. The average popular melody is of very simple construction and seems to welcome elaborate accompaniments, backgrounds, and figurations. These devices are sometimes developed to such an extent that they assume an importance almost equal to that of the melody. An accompaniment that enhances the melody, and is interesting in itself, has great value to the arranger. Properly used, it can serve as a strong cohesive element to the whole arrangement by being a source of material for the introduction, modulations, transitions, and ending. In the arrangement of Rumbolero, a simple rhythmic figure is used for the introduction, transitions, ending, and in one form or another continues uninterruptedly throughout the entire number.

Figure motive:　　Ex. 240

Introduction:

Accompaniment to first theme:

Transition:

Accompaniment to second theme. (Rhythmic modification)

Transition:

Transition. (Rhythmically modified.)

Accompaniment to first theme:

Final statement of first theme:

Ending:

Final Ending:

Ex.250

In the arrangement of Moszkowski's Bolero a similar rhythmic motive is deployed with the same technique. This one bar rhythmic fragment, in various guises, recurs throughout the entire number.

Ex. 251

Motive:

Introduction:

Ex.252

Accompaniment to 1st Theme:

Ex.253

Transition:

Accompaniment to 1st Theme:

Modified accompaniment:

Ending:

Generally speaking, the beginning arranger creates far too much unrelated material. As illustrated above, one thoughtfully created, extracted, or constructed idea will serve as a source of material for a whole arrangement. Careful use and exploitation of a few devices will create an arrangement of clarity, cohesion, and sustained interest. Lavish use of unrelated ideas and devices can only present a picture of confusion, and instability; an "up and down" feeling. **WP 46**

Every composition has within its component elements characteristic rhythms, harmonic progressions, or melodic fragments, that can be elaborated and developed into a pattern or accompaniment figure, serving as a basic idea for all, or part, of the material necessary to round out the form of an arrangement. In the arrangement of "American Salute" the rhythmic pattern of the melody is the source of material for the introduction, accompaniments, figurations, and ending.

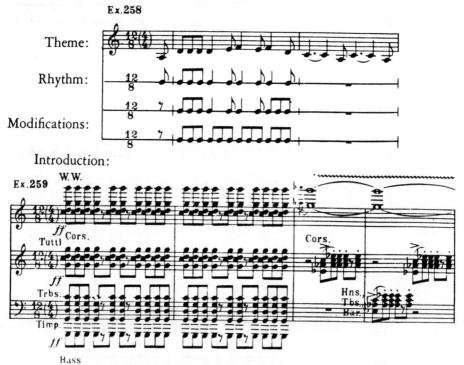

Accompaniment to theme:

Ex.260

Accompaniment to theme:

Ex.261

Accompaniment to theme:

Ex.262

Rhythm of melodic variation:

Ex.263

Transition:

Ending:

This elaboration of thematic material in whole or part, either melodically, rhythmically, or harmonically, is a fundamental device of the composer. It is equally important to the arranger who must develop the facility of creating and assembling these motives from the original material. Once these motives have been extracted they must be deployed and instrumentated with skill and taste. **WP 47**

Not all motives are so consistently used and others undergo greater modification and more fragmentary usage. In "Do-Si-Do," motives of the first theme and its rhythm, are utilized in a less obvious fashion.

1st Theme:

The rhythm of the first bar of this theme is the basis of the accompaniment for the second theme.

and later —

The pattern of the first theme in bar three is used as a motive for the start of the transition.

The first theme is again apparent as a motive in the coda.

The first theme in its entirety is used as a countermelody against the second theme in the last section of the number.

Ex. 271

In the arrangement of Rachmaninoff's Second Concerto, which was transcribed from the original orchestra score, the only added material is the introduction and ending. To keep this material in the style of the composer and unify the arrangement, the main theme was used as a source for these additions.

Ex. 272

Theme:

Ex. 273   Maestoso ($\bf{\mathit{d}} = 60$)

Introduction:

Ex. 274

Ending:

The identical procedure was used in writing the introduction and ending for the arrangement of Chopin's Polonaise. **WP 48**

Theme:

Ex.275

Introduction:

Ex.276   Cors.,Tpts

Ending:

Ex.277

As stated previously, all material created by the arranger must have some relationship to the melody, rhythm, or harmony of the original composition. However, quite often material related only to style, atmosphere, period, or story of the composition is preferred to thematic development. In the arrangemen of "School Days" material based on the nursery rhyme "London Bridge is Falling Down" is used to immediately suggest the atmosphere and locale indicated by the title.

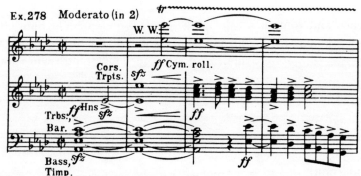

Ex.278 Moderato (in 2)

In like manner, to suggest the atmosphere and setting of a square dance, the introduction of "Do-Si-Do" is based on the sounds of a country fiddler turning his instrument.

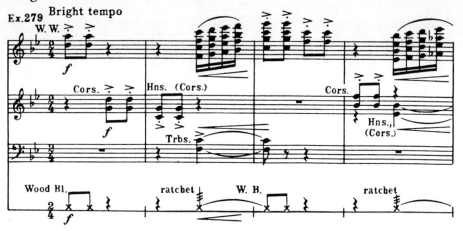

Ex.279 Bright tempo

PIANO LITERATURE:

The voluminous literature of the piano is an almost inexhaustible source of excellent material for band arrangements. In this repertoire are compositions of every style, form, and emotion. The selection of this material, like the selection of orchestral material for transcription, is largely a matter of taste. However, the very nature of some piano compositions, like those of the impressionistic school, renders them unsuitable for band or orchestral arrangements. Furthermore, virtuoso works replete with pianistic technique, almost forbid any attempt at instrumentation. The skilled and inventive arranger can, it is true, devise a solution for practically every problem. But in so doing, he exhibits only lack of taste in distorting the composers' intentions.

Inherent form is a basic part of this literature. Unlike the 32 bar entity of a popular song, works for the piano (even in the small song forms), are created with a definite thematic construction that is an integral part of the composition. Except for an occasional elaboration of the beginning or ending, the sequence and content of the material should remain intact. There is no need for the alteration of themes, or creation of modulations or transitions. This technique is used only in arranging popular material òr when the material is so fragmentary that the arranger must create his own form.

In this type of scoring the creative contribution of the arranger is limited to the solution of pianistic technique and the assignment of instrumentation and color. Unlike orchestral material, this literature was created solely for the piano and exhibits no instrumental color. Within these limitations the arranger has full freedom in accordance with his taste and skill.

In Part 3 the fundamental approach to scoring simple piano works was discussed. While the majority of examples in the exposition of this subject were of popular music, the principles advanced will apply to all piano compositions in the smaller forms. The devices of accompaniments, countermelodies, and figurations should be reviewed so that they may be quickly recognized in the literature of the piano. **WP 49**

The General Procedure of Scoring should again be followed. After the material has been selected, the greatest part of the arranger's technique will be utilized in consideration of step 2, Form. As stated previously, this consideration of form, in direct opposition to arranging popular music, is now analytical and not creative. When the component elements of the composition have been analyzed they should be lettered, or numbered, and instrumentation assigned. The steps of key consideration, condensed score, and full score follow in regular order, with no change in their application or technique.

Like the transcription of the orchestral strings, the chief concern in arranging piano literature is an understanding of the technique and notation peculiar to the instrument. The right hand of the pianist is the soprano and alto voice, and the left hand is the tenor and bass. More specifically the right hand plays the melody, and the left, the accompaniment. An understanding of the technique of the left hand, and the way its music is notated, is of fundamental importance.

In fulfilling its assignment the left hand is frequently taxed in expressing the rhythmic and harmonic elements of the accompaniment. As the performer of the bass voice, the left hand is responsible for this, plus the harmonic accompaniment in its proper rhythmic form. Having but five fingers for the execution of these elements, the notation is such that the individual components are not always readily apparent. The arranger, working with the basic elements of composition, melody, harmony, rhythm, (bass) is concerned with the isolation of these elements for instrumentation. Accompaniments in a basic form readily exhibit component parts and can be instrumentated without modification.

Ex.280

The basic accompaniment elements of rhythm, harmony, and bass line are obvious in the above examples. No modification is needed and they plainly suggest instrumentation to the arranger.

Accompaniments suggesting sustained harmony, plus a rhythmic movement are more difficult for the arranger to recognize.

Ex.281

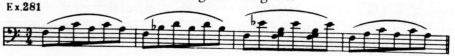

On first analysis, bars 1-2 and 4 of Ex. 281 seem to be single line accompaniments of a rhythmic nature. Further analysis indicates that they also spell out the harmonic structure. However, since this is piano music, the slur is the strongest indication of the nature of the accompaniment. This slur over each bar indicates that these groupings are to be played legato, and on the piano, this will sustain each note beyond its time value. The implication of the slur, in the technique of piano, is as follows:

Ex.282

WRITTEN   ACTUAL SOUND   EFFECT

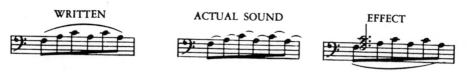

The rhythm and harmonic structure has now been isolated and only the bass line is needed to complete our analysis. As the bass is always the lowest voice the "F's" in each bar are the bass line. A glance at the third bar will prove that this is the case as the composer has here indicated that he wanted three bass notes. If he desired only one bass note, as in bars 1-2 and 4, he probably would have notated the passage as follows:

Ex.283

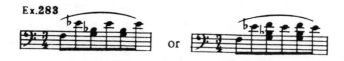

Our analysis has isolated the elements of this accompaniment and shows that there are three related parts. Expressed individually, they are now available for instrumentation.

This legato quality of the piano must be remembered when instrumentating piano accompaniments. A simple experiment of having bars 1 and 2 (Ex. 281) played on a clarinet and then a piano will prove that our analysis of three related parts is sound. The clarinet legato will be more rhythmic than harmonic as each tone will cease when the next is played. The piano quality will be equally rhythmic and harmonic as the legato quality of the instrument will sustain each note beyond its time value.

Basically, the analysis procedure of isolating the component parts will serve for all piano accompaniments exhibiting a flowing rhythmic and harmonic style. Related examples would be analyzed as follows: **WP 50**

Ex.287

Ex.288

Other accompaniments, while readily exhibiting component parts, are written in such a manner as to be unsuitable (in the original form) for instrumentation. The following examples are notated so that they are playable by the left hand with a minimum of skips and leaps. This construction, proper for the piano, is unsatisfactory for the arranger. The components are too closely related and the voicing, while correct, is too low, and not properly grouped for instrumentation. A higher position of the accompanying chords would permit better voice grouping and a clearer separation from the bass line.

Ex.289   **WP 51**

Original

Modification

Ex.290

Original

Modification

In performing full and climatic passages for the piano, comparable to the tutti of the band, the pianist is limited to what he can play with two hands. He accomplishes this by playing the extremes of the structure, top and bottom, revealing in between a large section of the harmonic structure that is not sounded. Furthermore, being limited to the scope of the fingers of each hand the voicing is too compact, particularly in the bass staff, for instrumentation.

Ex. 291 illustrates this type of writing. The large harmonic area not sounded must be filled in before scoring for the band. A tutti scoring of the passage in its present construction would have an all top and bottom sound. The tutti would also be weak as many soprano and alto instruments, (because of their compasses) could not be assigned to the passage.

In the bass staff the harmonic structure is entirely too close and if scored in its present form would have a very muddy sound. A revoicing, in accordance with the overtone series,[2] is necessary.

Ex. 292 illustrates the revoicing and addition required for proper instrumentation. The bass line has been strengthened by separation from the rest of the structure and a spreading and revoicing of the harmony now permits the assignment of the instruments of the full band. **WP 52**

Examples requiring similar treatment are illustrated below.

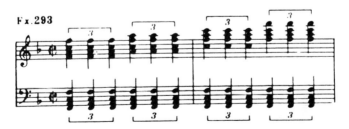

2. The arrangement of overtones (and their intervals) of the harmonic series is regarded as the proper distribution of intervals in harmonic construction. Large intervals in the lower voices (bass and tenor) and smaller intervals in the soprano and alto, assure clarity of structure.

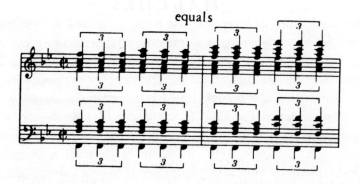

Ex.294

ORGAN AND CHORAL LITERATURE:

The band is admirably instrumentated, even more so than the orchestra, for the performance of organ and choral literature. The many reed choirs, single and double, along with the full brass, especially in the tenor, bass and contrabass register, offer a wealth of sympathetic colors and facilities for scoring this material.

Compositions for organ and chorus are largely contrapuntal and seldom exhibit more than four or five voices. Our original quartet approach to scoring for band, with its instrumental and vocal relationship, is the ideal technique for arranging these works.

Except for some organ works, this literature seldom indicates any preference of instrumental color and the arranger is unrestricted in scoring. The keys of this material may be changed, subject to the demands of the arranger's instrumental color and structure. Form, however, is an integral part of these compositions, and, except for the smaller pieces, is scored without any additions, deletions, or modifications. **WP 53**

The band, from its inception, has been recognized as the ideal marching ensemble. Social, community, and military affairs requiring music of spirit, volume, and mobility, are admirably suited to its instrumentation. The tremendous growth and popularity of the band in America is directly traceable to its use as a connecting link between the school and the community. In its symphonic instrumentation the band is the leader of instrumental school music and regularly appears in performances of concert music. For sports activities, community affairs, parades, etc., it exhibits a different instrumental composition and repertoire. This split personality is both a liability and an asset to the band and the successful director is the one that approaches each ensemble with a different viewpoint, instrumentation and literature.

All these viewpoints are equally important to the composer and arranger. With the marching band, its instrumentation is our first concern. The instrumental composition of this ensemble is largely dictated by the portability of instruments and their ability to play outdoors. As a result, it is necessary to alter the symphonic instrumentation by eliminations, additions, and substitutions. Ex. 295 illustrates a comparison of the symphonic and marching band instrumentation.

Ex. 295

SYMPHONIC BAND	MARCHING BAND
Piccolos (D-flat and C)	Piccolos (D-flat and C)
Flutes	Flutes
Oboes[3]	O
E-flat Clars.	E-flat Clars.
B-flat Clars.	B-flat Clars.
Alto Clars.	Alto Clars.
Bass Clars.[4]	Bass Clars.
Contra Bass Clars.[5]	O
Bassoons[3]	O
Contra Bassoons[5]	O
Saxophones[5]	Saxophones
Cornets	Cornets
Trumpets	Trumpets
Horns (F and E-flat)[6]	Horns (E-flat)
Baritones	Baritones
Trombones	Trombones
Basses (B-flat and E-flat)[7]	Basses (E-flat)
Timpani[5]	O
Percussion	Percussion (Sn. Dr., Bass Dr., Glockenspiel)

3. Oboes and bassoons are delicate instruments not practical for marching bands.
4. Bass clarinets are awkward to carry and are only occasionally used.
5. Contra bass clarinets, contra bassoons, bass saxophones and timpani are not portable.
6. Horns are delicate instruments and their circular valve mechanism is easily affected by weather. It is a general practice to use mellophones as substitutes.
7. E-flat basses are substituted for B-flat basses which are very heavy and awkward to carry. (This is a consideration in scoring marches because of the different compasses of these instruments.)

The marching band includes only those instruments that are portable and can function outdoors. The uses of this ensemble, the music it plays, and its style of playing is equally functional and dictated by practical considerations.

Adequate volume is a basic necessity. The band must be heard. Without the acoustics and resonance of the concert hall the instruments have to be regrouped for the maximum volume of sound.

Considerably more emphasis is placed on rhythm. Band music has a very elemental physical attraction. To provide a strong rhythmic cadence to physically inspire marching units, as well as itself, the rhythm instruments and the rhythmic components of the music are emphasized. While the reeds are included in the ensemble, the marching band is fundamentally brass and percussion. The instruments of the marching band in the order of their importance, and listing their basic functions, are as follows:

Ex. 296

1.	Cornets, Trumpets	Melody (unison or harmonized)
2.	Percussion	Rhythm
3.	Trombones, Baritones, Saxophones	Harmony, Countermelodies Rhythm
4.	Basses	Rhythm
5.	Horns	Melody (unison or harmonized)
6.	Reeds	Figurations

The division of voices, contrast of instrumental tone, elaboration of accompaniments, and other devices of scoring have obviously little place in the technique of scoring for this ensemble. Due to the absence of many color instruments, and the necessity for volume, the marching band exhibits very little contrast of color. As a substitute (and very effective) it presents a strong contrast of dynamics. Much unison writing, for entire sections, is necessary for the effective presentation of melodies and countermelodies. Accompaniments are models of simplicity and preponderantly rhythmic. Functionally, the basis components of a march (as exemplified in Ex. 296) are in the following proportion: 2 parts melody, 1 part harmony or countermelody, and 3 parts rhythm. This is indicative of the superiority of rhythm and melody over the harmony. Actually the harmony is the third consideration as a marching unit of cornets, trumpets, and percussion (personified by the very popular drum and bugle corps) is extremely effective. The addition of trombones and baritones, supplying harmony or countermelodies (also largely rhythmic), completes the three basic elements of music; melody, harmony, and rhythm.

An analysis of a Sousa march will illustrate the simple and direct presentation of these elements.

A unison introduction for tutti band is a familiar device of the great march composers and as a means of commanding attention is unsurpassed. The melodic line has a very pronounced rhythmic pulse and from the very first note establishes a definite cadence.

Scored for reeds (clarinets divisi) and unison cornets and trumpets (baritones 8 basso), the melody (Ex. 298) is given a very strong presentation. The balance of the band sounds the harmonic structure emphasizing the rhythm of the melody.

Ex. 299 is a continuation of the previous strain and illustrates the use of dynamic contrast. The melodic instrumentation is the same while the horns are now assigned to rhythm. The trombones and low saxophones are harmonic and rhythmic.

In Ex. 300 the cornets and trumpets are harmonized (and naturally weakened) but are strengthened by the reeds in unison. The trombones and low saxophones have a strong countermelody and the horns are still assigned to rhythm.

The cornets, trumpets and baritones (8 basso) (Ex. 301) are again in unison; the trombones harmonized and rhythmic; the horns rhythmic, and the woodwinds have a figuration in unison. All elements are clear cut and distinctive and the balance is such that none overshadows the other.

This "break" strain Ex. 302 (derived from the preceding theme) is extremely powerful and exhibits a contrast of tone, mainly by an exchange of registers.

This composition is not a haphazard selection. It represents the simplicity and directness of all marches of Sousa as well as those of the other great march composers. In opposition to marches scored in symphonic style, and inadequate for outdoor performance, the works of these composers were created for field use, but are applicable for concert performance. It is the scoring conception that makes a composition a good march.

The formula (and there is a formula) for the effective scoring of marches is obvious in the previous Examples 297 to 302. It will be noticed that at no time are the most numerous instruments of the band; clarinets, cornets, trombones, simultaneously divided. The fundamental conception of the band as composed largely of these three sections limits the maximum number of simultaneous ideas to three, and provides sufficient strength for an effective presentation of each.

In Ex. 298 the clarinets and trombones are divided and the cornets in unison. The melody is scored for divided clarinets (reeds) and unison cornets. If the cornets were divided the melodic presentation would be considerably weaker as two-thirds of these instruments would then be playing harmony. The harmonic structure is effectively sounded by the trombones and clarinets and there is no point in weakening the melody to reinforce this, already strong, element.

In Ex. 300 the melody is scored for divided cornets and unison reeds, with the trombones on a countermelody. As the trombones are in unison it is necessary that the cornets be divided to provide the harmonic structure. This division of the cornets weakens the melody necessitating the use of reeds in unison for reinforcement.

In Ex. 301 the clarinets and cornets are in unison and the trombones again divided. If the figuration for reeds were harmonized (divided) the volume of this idea would be insufficient for effective outdoor presentation.

This viewpoint of the marching band as composed essentially of three instrumental sections is sound and practical, and if used as an approach to this type of scoring will always produce effective results. It must not be felt that this approach is so basic as to prevent or limit the creation or development of ideas. The elements of Melody, Harmony, and Rhythm, plus the devices of figuration and countermelody, when deployed for the three instrumental sections present countless scoring possibilities. The chart below lists but a few of these combinations.

Ex. 303

Piccs., Fls.	Melody	Melody	Figuration	Harmony	Melody
Clarinets.	(div.)	(unis.)	(unis.)	(div.)	(div.)
Cornets	Melody	Melody	Harmony	Counter	Melody
Trumpets	(unis.)	(div.)	(div.)	(unis.)	(unis.)
Trombones	Harmony	Counter	Melody	Melody	Counter
Baritones	(div.)	(unis.)	(unis.)	(unis.)	(unis.)

It is apparent from the Sousa examples and the above chart that the symphonic and marching bands are two different ensembles. The instrumental structure and musical purpose of each is such that these ensembles demand a different technique in the creation and scoring of their material. Music for marching bands should be simple and direct. The melodies should be tuneful and the whole must have a strong rhythmic pulse. A large portion of marches, as well as other material for marching bands, is actually unsuitable for outdoor performance. This material is still being conceived symphonically, both in style and instrumentation, and has little value to the marching band. **WP 54**

The rhythmic conception of symphonic writing is similarly impracticable for marching bands. Horns playing rhythmic chords are effective in the concert hall due to helpful acoustics and a minimum of percussion. Outdoors their tone is quickly dissipated and they are outnumbered by percussion instruments of great volume. The horns cannot compete with, and hardly assist, the percussion in providing rhythm. Along with this their harmonic contribution is negligible and they should be otherwise employed to make any contribution.

Furthermore, it is the policy of contemporary bands to march much faster than in the past (sometimes as fast as 180) making it practically impossible for a brass or reed instrument to play rhythm. At a fast cadence simple rhythmic figures as,

Ex.304

are impractical. This is the function of percussion who have ample volume and can execute cleanly.

Reference to Ex. 299 will illustrate the need for a better use of the horns. This is the customary conception of the use of these instruments and they are well scored. However, they actually make little, or no contribution to the arrangement. They are supporting the rhythmic pattern of the melody, as are the drums, but the drums are much more effective. Harmonically, they are hardly needed as the strong trombone section is sounding the harmonic structure and more harmony is offered in the clarinet division.

This is not to say that the horns are unnecessary in the marching band, but rather that they are ineffectively employed. In the same example they would make a much greater contribution if they were scored with the trombones.

Similarly, in Ex. 300 the horns are duplicating rhythms and harmony much more effectively presented by other instruments; cornets and drums.

Here the horns would be better employed on the melody (8 basso) or again scored with the trombones.

This ineffective employment of horns, along with other practices patterned after symphonic scoring, has resulted in an increasing demand by band leaders for a new approach to scoring marches. Failing to get any attention they have been making what modifications they can with present material by eliminating some parts, reassigning others, etc. This is largely a futile attempt as these methods, with the present scoring conception, will produce nothing but distortion.

The demand for a new approach or conception to material for the marching band is understandable in the light of the special function of this ensemble. It is the composers and arrangers (not bandleaders) who should experiment with this instrumentation in an effort to devise a system of scoring (having no bearing on the symphonic technique) that will best serve the needs of the marching band.

The author has done much experimentation in this type of scoring and is presently preparing a series of marches, and other material, for marching bands. The scoring is based on a new approach to the instrumentation of this ensemble as well as a more practical view of its specialized functions. In the evolution of this technique the suggestions of bandleaders were solicitated, tried, and incorporated. The format that emerged was the result of experiments covering the following major points.

Ex. 305 (1)   Simplified instrumentation.

(2)   Division of voices.

(3)   Fewer parts.

(4)   Rhythm.

SIMPLIFIED INSTRUMENTATION:

In discussions with leading University, College, and High School Band leaders it was proved that the marching band instrumentation (reduced from the symphonic band (Ex. 295) is substantially correct. However, they all recommend still further simplification.

Flutes are seldom used in marching bands and these instrumentalists are assigned to piccolos. With the piccolos the D-flats outnumber the C's four to one. The small E-flat clarinet is rare in symphonic bands and is nonexistent in marching units. The alto and bass clarinets are very rarely used and all concerned advise their elimination. The saxophones are quite popular except the baritone which is seldom used due to its size and weight. Lyre bells (Glockenspiel) are also very popular and the average band has at least two and sometimes many more. The balance of the band from cornets to basses is to be retained as is.

Incorporating these points the marching band instrumentation is now as follows:

Ex. 806

D-flat Piccolos
B-flat Clarinets
Saxophones (Alto, Tenor)
Cornets (Trumpets)
Horns "F"
Horns "E-flat"
Baritones
Trombones
Basses
Drums
Lyre Bells

DIVISION OF VOICES:

The symphonic technique of dividing the three large instrumental sections into three voices (Clars. 1-2-3, Cornets 1-2-3, etc.) is necessary and sound. The seating arrangement and the helpful acoustics of the concert hall all assist in balancing these voices even if the number of instruments is relatively small.

For marching bands this three part division is weakening in the extreme and deprives the band of its much needed impact. A band of fifty players will average twelve to fifteen cornets and trumpets. This division would assign only a third of these instruments (four or five) to the melody, insufficient for a band of this size in outdoor performance.

This same deduction can be applied to the other sections of the band usually written in three voices. The clarinet tone is quickly dissipated outdoors and divided by three they are even more ineffective. Further, this division occasionally leads the second and third instruments into a register where they have very little volume of tone even under ideal conditions.[8] The trombones are less numerous than the cornets, and while they are seldom assigned to the melody, any scoring for these instruments is weakened when written in three parts.

A division by two, instead of three, is indicated for these three major sections to retain sufficient power for outdoor performance. Such a division when applied to the major brasses gives five strong voices (cornets, two voices; trombones, two voices; and basses, one) sufficient for the presentation of any harmonic structure. Writing the reeds in two voices (also octaves) greatly strengthens their effectiveness when reinforcing the melody or presenting figurations.

8. Ex. 298 third clarinets.

FEWER PARTS:

The division of the major instrumental sections into a maximum of two voices presents the possibility of eliminating a great many parts in a marching band arrangement. The standard publication includes a separate part for each of the 1st, 2nd, and 3rd clarinets, cornets and trombones. As it is quite possible, and readable, to have two voices on a part, we will write only one part for each of these sections. Other parts can be eliminated by utilizing the similarity of functions of the tenor saxophone and treble clef baritone; bass clef baritone and trombones; alto saxophones and E-flat horns.

Experimentation has shown that these deductions are sound and practical and it has been proved in performance that an effective marching band arrangement can be scored for a maximum of ten separate instrumental parts.[10]

Ex. 307

(1)	D-flat Piccolo	one part	one voice
(2)	B-flat Clarinets	one part	unison or two voices
(3)	Cornets (Trumpets)	one part	unison or two voices
(4)	Horns "F"[11]	one part	two voices
(5)	Horns "E-flat"[11] E-flat Alto Sax's.	one part	two voices
(6)	B-flat Tenor Sax. Treble Clef Baritone	one part	one voice
(7)	Trombones Bass Clef Baritone	one part	unison or two voices
(8)	Basses	one part	one voice
(9)	Drums	one part	
(10)	Glockenspiel Flutes	one part	

RHYTHM:

The usual inefficient employment of the horns has already been discussed. Due to their inability to compete with percussion, both in technique and volume, they will rarely be used for rhythm. For greatest value they will be scored to support the melody, harmony, or countermelody .

Application of these techniques to the foregoing Sousa march will show that even this excellent composition can be better scored for the needs of the marching band.

In Ex. 298 the cornets are assigned the melody in unison. The clarinets are divided into three voices with the third voice in a register that is the weakest on the instrument. There are four voices for the trombones and baritones some of which are duplicating the bass and melody. A sketch of this example with a maximum of two voices for the three main instrumental sections is as follows:

10. These are duplicated to provide sufficient parts for all players.
11. The horn parts in F and E-flat are the same differing only in transposition.

Ex.308

The harmonic structure is complete, well balanced, and well voiced. The clarinets have been strengthened by the omission of the third voice, dividing their numbers between into two voices, both of which are in a good register. The duplications in the trombones and baritones have been eliminated and these instruments (supported by the basses) now sound a much stronger harmonic structure as there are adequate numbers on each voice. The assignment of saxophones and horns can best be exemplified by a full scoring of the passage.

Ex.309

Bandleaders are enthusiastic in their acceptance of this technique. Aside from the functional value of these scoring modifications they are quick to point out many other, and more practical, advantages. As all superfluous parts are eliminated and each player has a part of basic importance, the morale is higher. A single part for each of the three major sections simplifies the distribution of parts as well as enabling the bandleader to balance on the field (without an exchange of parts) the instruments in each section. Lastly, this set-up of parts is more practical to the bandleader as all are assigned, and he does not purchase parts that are not used.**WP 55**

It is to be expected that further experiments will indicate changes in this technique and the set-up of parts and the arranger is invited to exercise his inventiveness. The initial reaction to these experiments is so encouraging as to indicate that a functional scoring for the marching band will stem from this basic approach.**WP 56**

SOLOS:

Scoring for solo instruments and band does not involve any techniques other than those already discussed. The devices of accompaniments, counter-melodies, and figurations, as advanced in Part 3 of this text, constitute almost the entire approach to his type of scoring.

A solo instrumentalist, accompanied by band, is to be viewed in the same light as an accompanied solo instrument in a symphonic band arrangement. The type and activity of the accompaniment, as well as its balance and quality of tone, should be contrived and selected to support and enhance the solo passage. The devices of countermelody and figuration are employed in accordance with the accompaniment need for added interest, instrumental color, and rhythmic activity.

In scoring solo or soli passages in a symphonic arrangement, instrumental assignments are made after careful consideration of those instruments having the ability to play the passage. Here the passage is the given quantity and instrumentation is assigned in accordance with its demands.

In scoring for a solo instrument and band the procedure is reversed. Here the solo instrument is the given quantity and the material is selected, transposed, modified, etc., for its most effective presentation.

Band literature abounds with solos for cornet, clarinet, trombone and baritone. Mere mention of these instruments will recall to mind many examples of this type of writing and there is no need of any further explanation. The majority of these compositions are of the theme and variation form designed to exploit and display technical virtuosity. The accompaniment is subordinate in the extreme, usually with little or no instrumental color; mainly an "oom pah" background with an occasional bombastic tutti calculated to revive the lagging interest of the accompanying players.

The author feels that this type of solo writing is of the same vintage as the "Silver Cornet" bands; to be revered, but not perpetuated. Solo material should be selected and treated as an arrangement, with less obvious and more musical deployment of thematic structure and instrumental devices. There are tremendous possibilities for the creation of solo material in the vast instrumental and vocal literature, both classical and popular. The accompaniment should not be treated as a thing apart. While necessarily subordinate to the solo it should be scored with all possible interest and color.

Every instrument of the band can be a soloist and in addition to the above instruments the reader is urged to consider those less frequently used. Solos for flute, oboe, alto and bass clarinet, saxophones, and horn would contribute greatly to the variety of programs. Preparation of special material for the more rare of these instruments as oboe, bassoon, and alto clarinet would do much to interest beginners in them, and facilitate their better representation in the band.

Perhaps the most colorful solo instruments are those most rarely used, particularly instruments of the keyboard type. The xylophone, vibraphone, marimba, piano, accordion, and harp possess great visual interest and instrumental color. Aside from creating special arrangements for these instruments, suitable settings can be devised by slight editing of published material. Examination of a few condensed conductor scores will illustrate the possibility of devising an accompaniment for a solo keyboard instrument by simply tacciting a few parts. The following example is an extract of a few bars of the condensed score of "Bolero" by Moszkowski.

Ex. 310   1st Cls., E♭ Cl.

By simply marking tacet the melody instruments, B-flat and E-flat clarinets, and assigning the melody to a keyboard instrument a very effective solo arrangement can be devised. As indicated below the arrangement now becomes an accompaniment to any one of the solo instruments.

Ex. 311

Piano

Xylophone
Marimba
Accordion

Band

In like manner the instruments assigned to the melody in the following extract of "El Relicario" could be marked tacet and the melody given to a solo marimba, xylophone, accordion, or piano.

Ex. 312

The popular and more lyrical melodies have equal possibilities and their arrangements are very simply edited to a satisfactory solo presentation.

Ex. 313

In the above example the melody, as it is, could be assigned to a xylophone, marimba, or accordion. For a piano it would be written for both hands and include more of the harmonic structure.

Ex. 314

Piano

This exposition should not be construed as the proper or desirable method of scoring solo arrangements. It is merely offered as a simple means of devising adequate arrangements for solo keyboard instruments from existing material in every band library. **WP 58**

WORK PROJECTS

WP

WORK PROJECTS
INSTRUMENTAL VOICES — PART TWO

WP 1 List (without reference to Ex. 1) the complete instrumentation of the band, with the keys of the instruments, and the clef, or clefs they use.

WP 2 List the instruments of the band under the headings of timbre; Reed, Double Reed, Brass, Percussion.

QUARTET WRITING

WP 3 With Ex. 136 as a guide, list the instruments of the band under the vocal register headings, one register to each instrument. Viz.

SOPRANO	ALTO	TENOR	BASS
Flute	E. Horn	French Hn.	Bassoon

WP 4 On full score paper write the sounding compass of each instrument and within this, indicate its vocal register classification. Viz. Alto Sax.

WP 5 With the procedure of Ex. 138 as a guide, score the choral (A) for the suggested quartets (B). Write the instruments in score order (S.A.T.B.), each on its own staff, with the proper clef and key signature.

(A)   BACH

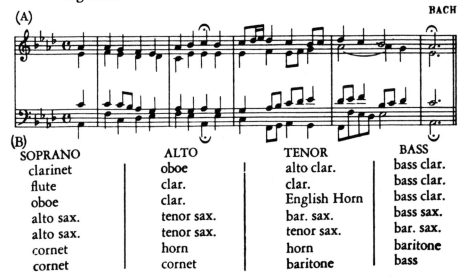

(B)

SOPRANO	ALTO	TENOR	BASS
clarinet	oboe	alto clar.	bass clar.
flute	clar.	clar.	bass clar.
oboe	clar.	English Horn	bass clar.
alto sax.	tenor sax.	bar. sax.	bass sax.
alto sax.	tenor sax.	tenor sax.	bar. sax.
cornet	horn	horn	baritone
cornet	cornet	baritone	bass

WP 6   Create new quartets (all reed or all brass) in the manner of WP 5B.
With this instrumentation score the choral A in WP 5.

WP 7   Score the choral below for the suggested quartets in WP 5B. Trans-
pose choral when necessary.

WP 8   Prepare from hymnals, or song books, quartets playable by members
of the class, groups of friends, or a band.

WP 9   As executed in Ex. 143, score the following choral for full band.
With Ex. 136 as reference, score all the soprano instruments on the
soprano voice, alto insts. on the alto voice, etc.

WP 10   Rescore the choral of WP 9 in the manner of Ex. 144, adding the
octave above the soprano (fls., piccs., etc.) the octave below the
bass (tuba, contra bassoon, etc.) and dividing the most numerous
instruments of the band between two voices. Do the same with the
chorals of WP 5 and WP 7.

WP 11   Select a hymn and score for full band.

WP 12   Score as many hymns, school songs, patriotic or popular songs as
possible for performance by small ensembles or full band, in concerts, rehearsals, assemblies, etc.

DIVISION OF VOICES

WP 13   Select numerous examples of quartet writing, hymnals, songs, etc. in open position and compress to closed position in the manner of Exs. 147 and 148.

WP 14   Continue the development of the examples of WP 13 by doubling the three soprano (treble) voices an octave lower in the bass clef (Ex. 144) and doubling the bass in octaves.

WP 15   Treat the following extract in the same manner as the textual presentation of "El Relicario" (Exs. 147 to 155). Follow the procedure of tutti scoring outlined in Ex. 158 making a *separate concert sketch for each step*. When all sketches have been completed, score for full band.

WP 16   With material selected from hymnals and folk song collections execute many more tutti scoring projects. Be very careful of steps 1 and 2 (Ex. 158) as each composition will require different treatment for the division of voices.

WP 17   Take the subjects of WP 12 and score for full band using the division of voices. Play these examples and also those of WP 12 to illustrate the development of scoring techniques.

ACCOMPANIMENTS

WP 18   Illustrate on a three staff score (Ex. 160) the three independent musical ideas (A-B-C) contained in popular piano music. Execute the first phrase (eight bars) of at least ten numbers to develop the habit of mentally recognizing these basic elements.

WP 19   Using the examples of WP 18, experiment with instrumentation for brass in the manner of Ex. 161.

WP 20   Experiment with reed instrumentation using the examples of WP 18.

WP 21   To the results of WP 20, double the melody (with a reed instrument) in the octave above.

WP 22   Select one of the examples of WP 18 and score for full band using the procedure of Ex. 166. Play this example to show the development of its instrumentation after first playing the same example as executed in WP 19-20-21.

WP 23 Using one or more of the examples of WP 18 rescore with the melody in the tenor register.

WP 24 Rescore the examples of WP 18 with the melody in bass.

WP 25 Rescore the examples of WP 18 with the melody in alto.

WP 26 As exemplified in Ex. 171 graphically illustrate the rhythms of the examples of WP 18.

WP 27 Experiment with the rhythms of WP 26 as exemplified in Ex. 172.

WP 28 Continue these rhythmic experiments with folk tunes, marches, jingles, etc.

WP 29 Review the melodic and harmonic devices of passing tones, added tones, suspensions, anticipations, etc. (From another text.)

WP 30 With Exs. 179 to 184 as a guide, elaborate the harmonic components of the subjects of WP 18.

WP 31 Review the construction and use of countermelodies. Analyze selected orchestral, piano, and choral literature to develop immediate recognition of this device.

WP 32 Again using the examples of WP 18 add countermelodies (sustained tone, diatonic line, elaboration of inner harmonic lines, melodic imitation) that are fitting to the structure of the composition.

WP 33 Further review countermelodies and figurations with particular emphasis on the difference in construction and use. Re-analyze the material used in WP 31, paying particular attention to figurations.

WP 34 Add figurations (either thematic or original) to the results of WP 32. Be particularly careful in the inclusion of this device, that the type of figuration used (rhythmic, melodic, unison or harmonized) be suitable to the composition. Do not overlook the use of percussion in the creation of figurations.

WP 35 Review carefully all material relating to cues and cross-cueing. It is important that the reasons for, the use of, and proper indication of these notations be clearly understood. Analyze and study band and orchestra scores carefully for this notation.

WP 36 Study carefully examples 213 and 214. When scoring, always prepare a suitable cue for any important instrument in a "symphonic" instrument. Analyze the suggested instruments for cueing in example 214 in regard to the similarity of timbre, register, and quality of tone with the original instrument.

WP 37 Rescore, on full score paper, the results of WP 34 cueing and cross-cueing all important passages for symphonic instruments.

GENERAL PROCEDURE OF SCORING

WP 38 Mentally or verbally, in class or privately, select suitable material for band arrangements, using hymnals, song books, or popular piano material.

WP 39 Using the material of WP 38 analyze your selections for form of composition, noting main or subordinate theme, counter melody, figurations, etc.

WP 40 Make a condensed score of WP 37. Study examples of orchestra and band condensed scores, noting the detail and brevity of notation.

WP 41 Make full scores of these previous examples.

WP 42 Analyze in class or privately, band or orchestra scores for structural construction and scoring devices as exemplified in the summation of part 2.

TRANSCRIPTIONS

WP 43 Study example 230. In conjunction with this chart select one or more orchestral compositions that have been transcribed for band and compare the original orchestral score with that of the band transcription.

WP 44 From the scores of some classical composers (Haydn, Mozart, Beethoven, etc.) select passages and transcribe for band.

ARRANGEMENTS

WP 45 Study scores of orchestral material that have been transcribed for band and note the fidelity with which the transcriber scores the original material. Study band arrangements of popular material, semi or light classical compositions, and observe the freedom of approach and creative contributions of the arranger.

WP 46 Observe, in the works of great composers, the frugal use of material. The themes of the work are the source of counter melodies, figurations, and all devices that constitute the complete composition. This cohesion of ideas is extremely important in arranging.

WP 47 From the examples of WP 18 develop motives that can be used for counter melodies, figurations and accompaniment.

WP 48 Using the motive developed in WP 47 create introductions, endings and transitions.

PIANO LITERATURE

WP 49 Analyze piano composition (collected works of composers, folios, etc.) noticing completeness of form, as well as construction devices.

WP 50 From the piano works of Mozart, Chopin, Debussy, etc. extract accompaniment figurations and graphically isolate the elements as indicated by examples 284 to 288.

WP 51 Select one or more short sonatinas from the collection of Clementi and Mozart and arrange for full band.

WP 52 Select works for piano requiring a completion of harmonic structure (Exs. 291-294) and score for full band.

CHORAL LITERATURE

WP 53 Select one or more choral works and score for band.

MARCHES

WP 54 Analyze some of the best known marches of Sousa, Pryor, etc., for the instrumental distribution of the three main elements of Melody, Harmony, and Rhythm. Ex. 303.

WP 55 Rescore all, or part, of one of the marches analyzed in WP 54 for the instrumentation suggested in Ex. 307.

WP 56 Score a march (school song, folk tune, etc.) for full band using the instrumentation suggested in Ex. 307.

SOLOS

WP 57 From vocal collections with piano accompaniments (Schubert's "Songs Without Words," etc.) select a composition to be scored for solo instrument and band.

WP 58 Analyze condensed scores of band works for the possible creation of solos as exemplified in Exs. 310-314.

212

INDEX

(The numbers apply to pages)

MUSICAL EXAMPLES QUOTED

AMARYLLIS — by Joseph Ghys — arr. by Philip J. Lang
Copyright 1948 by Mills Music, Inc.
Ex. 3, 14, 44, 48, 187, 188

AMERICAN SALUTE — by Morton Gould — trans. by Philip J. Lang
Copyright 1943 by Mills Music, Inc.
Ex. 10, 18, 19, 27, 75, 96, 131, 132, 133, 258, 259, 260, 261, 262, 263, 264, 265

BOLERO (Spanish Dance) — by Moritz Moszkowski — arr. by Philip J. Lang
Copyright 1948 by Mills Music, Inc.
Ex. 119, 252, 253, 254, 255, 256, 257, 310, 311

BRASS BAND BOOGIE — by Philip J. Lang
Copyright 1947 by Mills Music, Inc.
Ex. 42, 200

DANSE from "The Golden Age"— by Dmitri Shostakovich — arr. by
Philip J. Lang
Copyright 1943 by Mills Music, Inc.
Ex. 4, 76

DARK EYES — by Philip J. Lang
Copyright 1948 by Mills Music, Inc.
Ex. 33, 38, 81, 109, 110

DO-SI-DO — by Philip J. Lang
Copyright 1949 by Mills Music, Inc.
Ex. 37, 49, 100, 103, 116, 122, 123, 124, 222, 266, 267, 268, 269, 270, 271, 279

EL RELICARIO — by Jose Padilla — arr. by Philip J. Lang
Copyright 1941 by Mills Music, Inc.
Ex. 5, 31, 32, 34, 54, 56, 60, 82, 108, 147, 148, 149, 150, 151, 152, 153, 154, 155, 185, 194, 198, 312

FUNICULI FUNICULA — by Luigi Denza — arr. by Philip J. Lang
Copyright 1947 by Mills Music, Inc.
Ex. 28, 45, 59, 69, 92, 106, 157, 173

GAY NINETIES OVERTURE — by Philip J. Lang
Copyright 1944 by Mills Music, Inc.
Ex. 15, 16, 21, 29, 36, 53, 63, 64, 130, 134

LA SORELLA — by L. Gallini — arr. by Philip J. Lang
Copyright 1942 by Mills Music, Inc.
Ex. 7, 11, 23, 74, 77, 83, 95, 113, 195, 199, 204

MISIRLOU — by N. Roubanis — arr. by Philip J. Lang
Copyright 1941 by Colonial Music Publishing Co., Inc. Used by permission.
Ex. 43, 91, 117

NARCISSUS — by Ethelbert Nevins — arr. by Philip J. Lang
Copyright 1947 by Mills Music, Inc.
Ex. 47, 101, 182, 183, 184, 190, 209, 210

NEW CHINA MARCH — Morton Gould — trans. by Philip J. Lang
Copyright 1943 by Mills Music, Inc.
Ex. 206

PAVANNE — by Morton Gould
Copyright 1938 by Mills Music, Inc.
Ex. 26

POLKA from "The Golden Age" — by Dmitri Shostakovich — arr. by
Philip J. Lang
Copyright 1943 by Mills Music, Inc.
Ex. 52

POLONAISE IN Ab — by F. Chopin — arr. by Philip J. Lang
Copyright 1945 by Mills Music, Inc.
Ex. 275, 276, 277, 313, 314

RACHMANINOFF'S SECOND CONCERTO — arr. by Philip J. Lang
Copyright 1946 by Mills Music, Inc.
Ex. 24, 30, 62, 66, 97, 272, 273, 274

RED CAVALRY MARCH — by Morton Gould — trans. by Philip J. Lang
Copyright 1943 by Mills Music, Inc.
Ex. 20, 65, 87, 118

RUMBALERO — by Camarata — trans. by Philip J. Lang
Copyright 1949 by Mills Music, Inc.
Ex. 46, 99, 111, 112, 129, 189, 207, 217, 221, 241, 242, 243, 244, 245, 246, 247, 248, 249, 250

SALUTE TO THE ALLIES — arr. by Philip J. Lang
Copyright 1944 by Mills Music, Inc.
Ex. 6, 13, 17, 35, 71, 72, 73, 78, 79, 88, 89, 93, 105, 145, 196, 205

SCHOOL DAYS FANTASY (Will D. Cobb-Gus Edwards) —
arr. by Philip J. Lang
Copyright 1906 by Gus Edwards Publishing Co. Renewed 1934 and assigned to Mills Music, Inc.
Ex. 41, 58, 84, 94, 128, 278

WASHINGTON POST MARCH — by John Philip Sousa —
arr. by Philip J. Lang
Copyright 1945 by Mills Music, Inc.
Ex. 297, 298, 299, 300, 301, 302, 308, 309

WAVES OF THE DANUBE — by J. Ivanovici — arr. by Philip J. Lang
Copyright 1947 by Mills Music, Inc.
Ex. 55, 70, 102, 127, 159, 160, 167, 168, 169, 170, 178, 179, 180, 181, 191, 192, 193

YANKEE DOODLE — by Morton Gould — trans. by Philip J. Lang
Copyright 1945 by Mills Music, Inc.
Ex. 12, 22, 25, 61, 67, 68, 80, 98, 156, 186, 201, 202, 203, 208, 211, 212, 216, 223, 224, 227

YULETIDE OVERTURE — by Philip J. Lang
Copyright 1944 by Mills Music, Inc.
Ex. 8, 9, 57, 86, 107, 146, 197